T0283339

World-Class Service

Dennis Opstal
Jean-Pierre Thomassen
Translated by Mischa Hoyinck & Robert Chesal

WORLD CLASS SERVICE

The **6 Rules** of Creating Exceptional Customer Experiences

Boom

Original title: *Topservice voor veeleisende klanten*. Published by Boom uitgevers Amsterdam, 2021

Editor: Wilma Schreiber, Schreib redactie
Cover design: Hans Roenhorst, H2R+
Layout: Coco Bookmedia
Translation: Mischa Hoyinck & Robert Chesal, Words Worth

ISBN 9789024463435
ISBN e-book 9789024463442
NUR 801

PREFACE

Increasingly, organizations are faced with demanding customers. This goes for public organizations, but also for health care organizations and commercial businesses. Customers tend to be better informed, more individualistic and highly critical, and less likely to accept bad or mediocre service or being told 'no'. Some industries are used to this type of customer, for example the high-end hospitality industry, and the luxury goods and services industries – 5-star hotels, expensive cars and jewelry. But now, other industries also find themselves dealing with such customers.

This book shows you, the customer service representative, how to deal with these customers when saying 'no' is not an option. Note that this book does not argue that you should be a doormat. Obviously, there are limits to customer centricity, and to what customers can or should expect. However, we do argue that you should roll out the red carpet, to ensure that the growing group of demanding customers receive World-Class Service, and keep returning to your organization for more.

We dedicate this book to all those who shed blood, sweat and tears every day to offer their customers World-Class Service, even when those customers set the bar really high. Enjoy the read! For questions and comments, or to submit an example of World-Class Service for demanding customers, please contact us on LinkedIn.

Dennis Opstal and Jean-Pierre Thomassen

REVIEWS

'Smoothly written, clearly designed, and by combining theory with many practical examples, the book comes to life and is anything but a tough read. The authors' enthusiasm for superior service jumps off the page. That's the hardest thing to achieve: getting world-class service into the DNA of employees, managers, and teams.'
Aftersales Magazine

'A practical book that you can use straight away. Some theory, but mostly lots of tips, examples, and how-to's. An easy-to-read management book for anyone who deals with customers, and relatable enough to appeal to anyone who is a customer. The examples are recognizable and give you a deeper understanding of the person on the other side of the desk. The book's main strength is that it guides readers in how to deal with demanding customers, and how to recognize demanding customers in specific situations.'
Management Tribune

'*World-Class Service* distinguishes itself from other books on service by focusing explicitly on the employee who has to provide world-class service. But it's also a good read for any service provider who's open to improving their way of working. Easy to read, with lots of practical tips and suggestions. The theory is clearly explained, devoid of academic language and illustrated by many examples.'
Rudy Kor, organizational advisor and management book author

'This book should be standard literature for everybody who works in the automotive industry. Service advisors should learn this book by heart before working in the front office.'
Matthias Stevens, Owner Streamline Consulting/ Business Development Manager

TABLE OF CONTENTS

Introduction

As an employee you deal with customers every day. Sometimes dozens, sometimes hundreds. You receive customers at your counter or reception desk, in your office, on the phone. Maybe you serve them in flight, or when they dine in your restaurant. You might call them customers, guests, clients, or patients; the name they go by depends on your industry. You already know the 'average customer' doesn't exist. Some people are easy to please. They're your undemanding customers, the ones you really can't go wrong with. In some industries, they're common. But no matter what line of work you're in, you'll always encounter at least a few demanding, or even extremely demanding, customers. Those who set the bar high and are proud of it. These are the customers we focus on in this book. We explore the best way to serve them.

Every private organization, public agency and commercial business has them: demanding customers. They expect a lot and their expectations get higher every time they experience better service in other industries. The internet and consumer watchdogs have made customers better informed, more assertive, more aware of their rights and more prepared to exercise them.

While some industries might have few demanding customers, there are lines of business where demanding customers are already the majority. We're talking about the industries with customers who are used to spending a lot of money, like 5-star hotels, Michelin-star restaurants, beauty salons, exclusive retail shops, art dealers, travel agencies, luxury car dealerships, airlines, accountancy firms and law offices. These organizations set themselves apart by charging high fees for high-quality services and products. If you work for that type of organization, you will have noticed that your customers have expectations that match the fees. Their standards are high, they're critical and demanding.

We know you have to bring your A-game to offer each of these customers a great experience every single day. It's an art. It's you who can make a difference by getting it right with these demanding and critical customers. If you succeed, your service can ensure that potentially dissatisfied or even furious customers go home completely satisfied. Your actions alone can do more than websites, forms, chatbots, customer rooms, procedures, managers, and so on. Customer service reps make a difference! You are your organization's public face. You can amaze the customer, show them a personal touch, leave them with the feeling they're special. You and your co-workers are actually the only ones who can do this. Customers are sensitive. They can tell whether you got up on the wrong side of the bed or not, how happy you are to go to work, how motivated you are to do your job, how much pleasure you take in offering demanding customers excellent service. That's your challenge, every day and with every new customer. And that's where you can make a difference.

Based on our experience, we know what it takes to deal with demanding customers. We've boiled it down to six practical rules which we present to you in this book. We hope they will motivate you to keep getting better at this art. We know you already do many things right. But just like pro athletes, you need to keep raising the bar. We hope this book gives you insight into your own strengths and the areas where you can still improve. What we hope for most of all, is to inspire you to strive for excellence in your service.

This book is divided into three parts. Part A describes the environment you work in. This starts with the demanding customer. What are their expectations and what makes them tick? Then, we move on to the choices that organizations like yours have made. What kind of service do they offer and what does this mean? And then we return to you, the one who can make a difference, day in and day out. We discuss your motivation and why helping customers in a memorable and special way can give you a lot of job satisfaction.

Part B describes the six rules of excellent customer service. In our view, they come down to an attitude of respect. We discuss those rules one by one. We illustrate each one with practical examples, and, where it's helpful, a roadmap too.

You can only offer your customers great service under the right conditions. Part C describes what kind of setting your employer needs to provide, to enable you to make a difference on a daily basis.

PART A

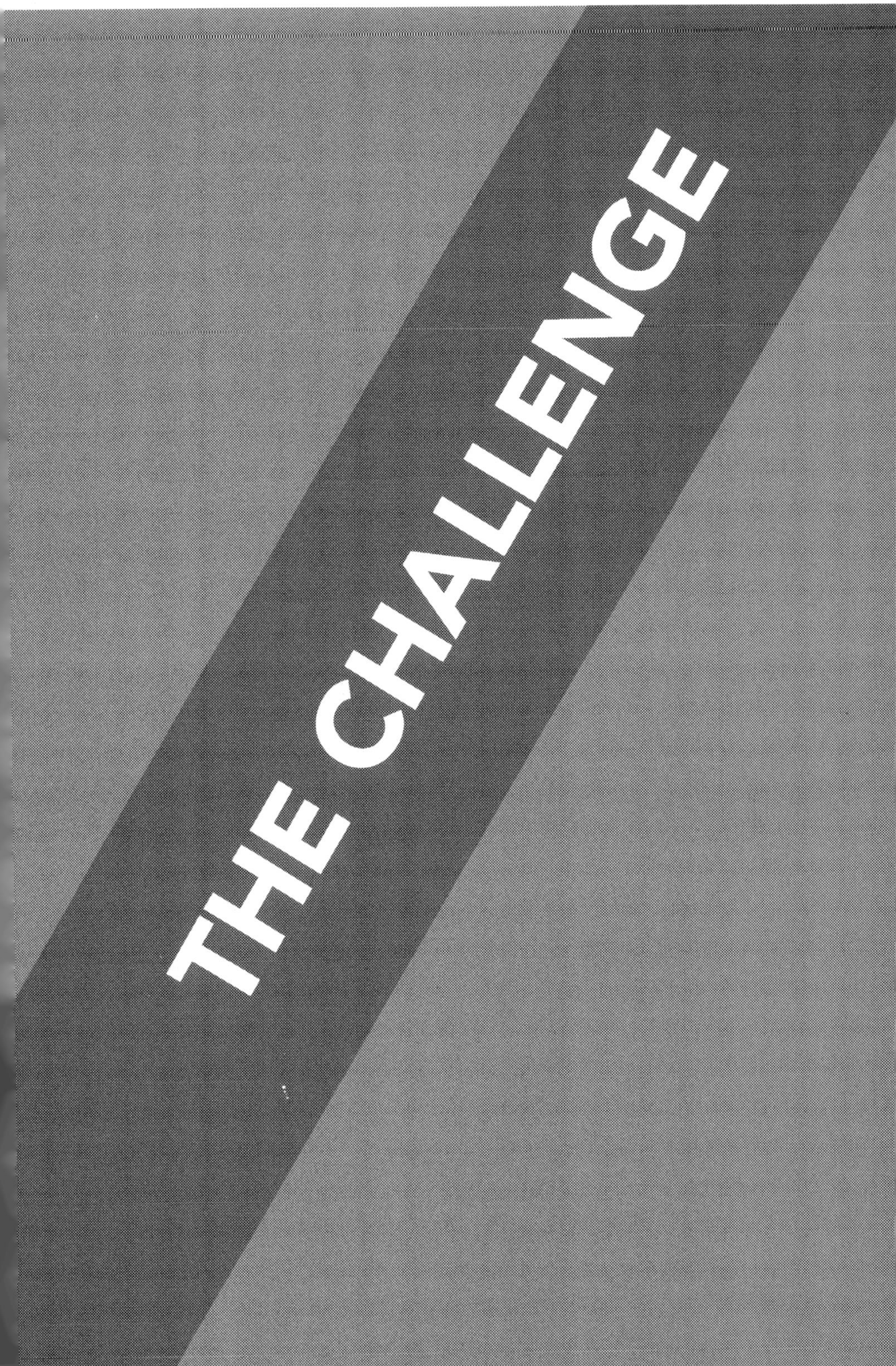
THE CHALLENGE

2 IT ALL STARTS WITH THE CUSTOMER

2.1. INTRODUCTION

Customers are the reason your organization exists. They're the reason you and your co-workers get paid. Without customers, there are no sales and no jobs. It's that simple. This is why it's important to take the customer journey as your starting point. Customers don't have to do business with your organization because they can go elsewhere. They're the ones who decide whether the experience you're offering them is extraordinary. They—and no one else—can judge whether your service is world-class. It all starts with them.

What are demanding customers? Why is there no such thing as an average customer? What are customer expectations and where do they come from? How does your service affect their experience and behavior? That's what this chapter is all about.

We believe that if you understand customers and why they act the way they do, you'll see why it makes sense to apply the six rules of excellent service.

2.2. DEMANDING CUSTOMERS

All organizations deal with a diversity of customers. This goes for business-to-business and business-to-customer organizations alike. Any organization's customer base can be divided into several groups. The simplest definition of a customer is: anyone who uses your products or services in any way. These are not just the people who already do business with your organization, but also the people who may do so in the future (your suspects and prospects). So if we widen our definition to include them, a customer is anyone who uses, or might someday use, your products or services. Obviously, this could also be an internal customer (a co-worker, business partner, dealer or vendor).

When we look at customer evaluations, we see that even though some customers feel the service was below par, they still give 3-, 4- and 5-star evaluations. They're forgiving, they reason that anyone can make a mistake, or they should have paid closer attention themselves. This shows that in many industries, most customers are easygoing and undemanding. But there's always a group of customers who set the bar really high, who are hard to please and require extra attention. What percentage of all customers are these so-called demanding customers? That varies a lot, depending on the organization you work for. How do you recognize them? Demanding customers have several behavioral characteristics and attitudes, and may display one or more of those described below:

- Accustomed to World-Class Service: customers who have much higher expectations than most. This may be because they (justifiably) attach expectations to the price of a product or service, or because they enjoy first-class service all the time and for them, great service is the norm.

- Attention seeking: customers who are hell-bent on taking up a lot of your time because they feel they deserve it, want reassurance, don't fully understand something about your product or service, are not truly independent, or personally have a great need for attention or information. They keep bending your ear and asking new questions.
- Bullying: people who believe only those who throw a few elbows around get their way. They do whatever they want, disregard the rules and have no respect for authority, you or other customers. They're often suspicious and argumentative. Some feel they should get whatever they demand because they're entitled to it! Still others are complainers and troublemakers, poised to be angry about one thing or another.
- Terrorizing: people with a chip on their shoulder, extremely dissatisfied and emotional, caught up in their own anger and sadness. Their complaints may or may not be unjustified. But in any case, these customers feel they've been wronged and they're furious about it.

Customers who are used to World-Class Service and have high expectations, expect to be treated like royalty. They set the bar really high, but as long as they get what they expect, they're happy. When something's off, however, they quickly get irritated and rude. They may let you know in no uncertain terms that they're displeased, they don't take kindly to being given the runaround. Before you know it, they're demanding to see the manager. Or if they write in to complain, they only want to deal with the CEO. If they feel they've been wronged, they can turn into real terrorists. These customers can take up a lot of your time and patience, but on the bright side, they also keep you on your toes and ensure that there's never a dull moment in your job.

How do you recognize these customers? Never by their appearances, only by their behavior. Mind you, there's no such thing as 'the average demanding customer', just like there's no average person, average German, average American, etc. Some behavior might be culture-related, but every customer is different. They each have their own pet peeves and reasons for them, their own wishes, expectations and preferences. If you want to offer World-Class Service to demanding customers, don't base yourself on misconceptions about 'the average' customer or customer segments, because you'll be basing yourself on prejudice. In the following chapters, you'll discover how you can make a difference based on the Number One rule: every customer wants to be treated according to their own preferences.

2.3. IT'S ALL ABOUT EXPECTATIONS

Train travelers expect the railway company to make sure the trains run on time. Diners want the restaurant to be able to serve what's on the menu. And if the restaurant is called 'Premium Lobster', they expect fresh lobster. Customers' basic expectations are not very complicated. If you want to serve demanding customers well, you need to know and understand their expectations. Let's start by looking at what these expectations are based on. There are five factors at play.

First of all, there's the organization's positioning. An organization that operates at a high price point creates different expectations than a budget organization. The greater the exclusivity, the higher the customer's expectations. A guest who pays 5000 euros a night at the Jumeirah Hotel in Dubai expects more than someone who checks into a motel for 85 euros a night. The second factor is previous experiences and precedents. Earlier encounters with

your organization or a similar service provider are very influential. Customers are quick to adjust their expectations upwards, so a perfect experience can easily become the norm. Conversely, they are slow to temper their expectations.
The third factor is your organization's communications. What promises does your organization make on its website, in ads and in conversation with customers? Customers expect you to make good on those promises. In 2017, United Airlines was embarrassed by a viral video of law enforcement officers forcibly removing a passenger from one of its planes. Just a few weeks later, the CEO sent all customers a letter in which he acknowledged that the company had broken the promise enshrined in the motto 'Fly the friendly skies.' His apology was necessary because the marketing slogan no longer reflected reality. The airline had told customers they could expect a high standard, and then failed to deliver. This is bound to lead to dissatisfaction and complaints.[1]
The fourth factor consists of what others say about your organization. Word of mouth has a powerful influence. Whether it's a recommendation from a friend or an online review from a stranger, it's impact on people's expectations can be great.
The fifth factor is the customer's personal characteristics. Their character, culture, religion, level of education and many other background specifics play a role in expectations.
Combined, these five factors determine each customer's personal expectation level. And clearly, demanding customers have higher expectations than average customers. Gaining insight into a customer's individual factors enables you to proactively cater to their particular expectation level.

The Kano model[2] below can help you understand customer expectations. This model distinguishes between customer expectations in terms of dissatisfiers (A), satisfiers (B) and delighters (C) (see Fig. 1).

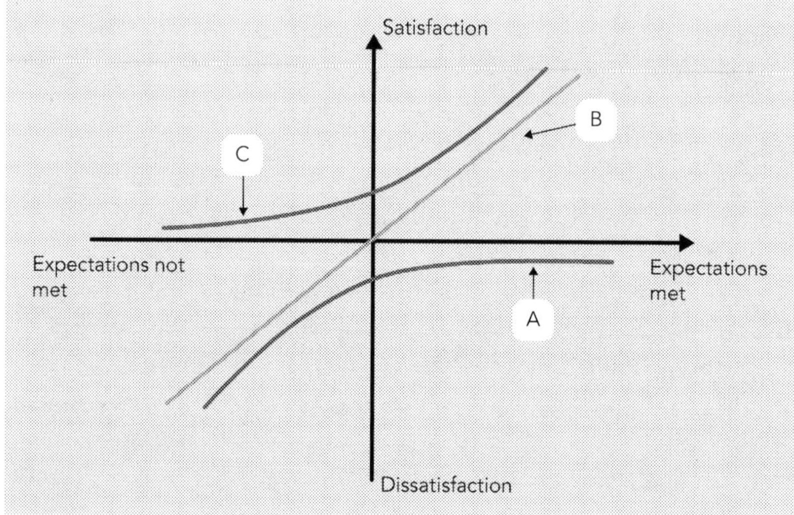

FIGURE 1. Dissatisfiers, Satisfiers and Delighters (Kano model)

Dissatisfiers (A) are basics that simply have to be delivered. They're what customers always expect. When they're delivered, it's no big deal and they have no impact on customer satisfaction. If they're missing, however, they quickly cause dissatisfaction. Examples of the basics that customers take for granted include: in hotels, they expect their room to be clean and the plumbing and A/C to work flawlessly; in restaurants, they expect the glasses to be polished, the food hot, the steak juicy and the wine at the right temperature. And when shopping online stores, they expect to be sent the products they ordered. These things don't make anyone extra satisfied, they're simply the bare minimum.

Satisfiers (B) are things that can have either a negative or a positive impact. If they're not as good as customers expect, they cause dissatisfaction; if they're better than expected, they can spark joy. The better they are, the happier the customers. For example, only having to wait five minutes for valet service is not bad, but immediate service is much better. Receiving a package sooner than expected increases satisfaction, receiving it later than promised causes dissatisfaction.

The third factor is the *delighters* (C): things that customers don't expect, but appreciate when they get them. They cause pleasant surprise when there, but no dissatisfaction when absent. Customers often don't even notice when they're missing. Think of a free upgrade to a nicer hotel room, a wireless charging point in your new car, or a bag of candy in the box of products you ordered online.

The problem, or rather the challenge, is that the distinction between dissatisfier, satisfier and delighter differs from customer to customer. One customer's delighter is another customer's dissatisfier. Take note, for demanding customers:

- services you provide can more readily become dissatisfiers because these customers place the bar higher;
- satisfiers – when missing – are more likely to have a negative impact;
- services you provide are less readily experienced as delighters.

Dissatisfiers, satisfiers and delighters

Dissatisfiers

1. All customers expect there to be a bed in their hotel room. A hotel room without beds would leave any guest dissatisfied.
2. Customers expect a taxi driver to know their way around. Drivers who have to stop and study Waze seem unprofessional.
3. Air travelers expect their luggage to arrive unscathed. Damaged suitcases cause dissatisfaction.

4. Car rental customers expect to be given a safe car that runs smoothly and has good tires and brakes. If they break down somewhere without cell phone coverage, they could flip.

Satisfiers

1. The faster luggage hits the belt after landing, the happier the traveler.
2. The shorter the wait in the checkout line, the better.
3. The easier customer service makes things for the online shopper, the more pleased the shopper will be.
4. The more convenient it is to drop off a rental car, the less stress the customer will experience.

Delighters (wow factors)

1. An air traveler gets an unsolicited upgrade to business class.
2. A customer's child gets a piece of candy from the store owner.
3. Hotel guests find a selection of fresh fruit in their room.
4. A rental car customer discovers a little gift in the car.
5. A customer plans to pick up a new model train track tomorrow, but an employee who happens to be in the neighborhood delivers it.
6. A customer gets a call from the maître d' who had said the restaurant was all booked up: "We have a table for you after all."

You should always keep in mind that your customers' expectations are likely to change. What is special today, will be the norm tomorrow. If a customer is checked in to their hotel room within two minutes of arrival, they will expect the same next time. If AAA arrives to give roadside assistance within ten minutes, the customer will consider that the norm.

The same goes for a free upgrade. Customers who get one, might count on getting one the next time, too. If their car has been cleaned and detailed, that might be a nice surprise this time, but they might be dissatisfied if that doesn't happen again on their following visit. Before you know it, a free upgrade or car wash has become a basic, and turns into a dissatisfier if it's not offered.

2.4. THE EXPERIENCE AND MOMENTS OF TRUTH

Everything customers see, hear, feel, taste and smell affects their experience. The customer experience is influenced by many factors: the impression your premises make, how you and your co-workers come across, your behavior, your organization's procedures, products and services. And the customer experience is quite subjective. A ten-minute wait can be awful, or no problem at all. Waiting ten minutes for some freshly cut, chilled melon while relaxing in a comfortable chair in the sun, sipping a drink, is a whole different experience than standing outside an IRS building in the pouring rain while waiting for the office to open. And ten minutes feels a lot longer when you're in a rush than when you've got all the time in the world. In short, customer experience is a personal reality and a personal perception, which means it can differ radically from your own reality, or your organization's.

Actually, every encounter between a customer and your organization is a moment of truth[3], a *Moment of Magic*[4]. It's a point in time when your organization can make or break its relationship with this customer. As a customer service representative, you can solidify the relationship by offering the customer a great experience. But you can also ruin it, by not taking a demanding customer seriously, for instance. If you go to YouTube and search for 'United Breaks Guitars', you'll see how that airline mismanaged a complaint from a customer whose guitar was destroyed by baggage handlers. United learned its lesson

the hard way: more than 21 million people have watched this viral video... But let's look at the bright side.
There's a TV consumer watchdog show in the Netherlands that doesn't just report on what goes wrong. It also gives businesses a thumbs up when they provide extra good service. The companies that get a special mention on the show are the ones whose customer service reps go the extra mile for their customers. Thankfully, there are many great examples of heart-warming customer service. Just google 'Ritz Carlton Joshie Giraffe' and see how a lost stuffed animal became world-famous.

Every customer service moment is a moment of truth, but there are four moments that stand out. To begin with, there is the first encounter. The first 30 or 40 seconds set the tone, and tell your customers whether things are headed in the right direction. Another key encounter comes at the end of the customer journey. Those final moments stay with the customer longest. Aside from the first and last moments, a third key moment is when a customer has a problem or complaint. We know from research that if you do a great job helping a customer in those situations, they'll end up more satisfied than if they had never had a complaint in the first place. This is called the Service Recovery Paradox, and we'll discuss it in more detail in Chapter 10. And finally, the fourth key customer service moment is when they experience particularly positive or negative emotions. All four of these moments warrant extra attention, because it's especially during these moments that you can make, or break, your organization's relationship with the customer.

Disney makes a sharp distinction between what it calls on-stage and off-stage worlds. Disney's visitors only ever get to see the on-stage world, the fantasy world that features Mickey and Minnie. They never witness the world behind the scenes, where

Mickey is just an ordinary guy or gal named David or Demi. If visitors did see Mickey undisguised, it would shatter the dream. On-stage, Peter Pan flies over a pirate ship with a wooden door with wrought-iron hinges and large rivets. Off-stage—on the inside—there's just a plain white door leading to a hallway and dressing rooms. The off-stage world is the world behind the scenes, where robotized characters are controlled. There are dressing rooms and cafeterias for the cast, and a control room full of screens where security guards monitor camera images from the park. This is where the products and services are prepared. This is where Elsa checks her make-up.

Your organization, too, has such an on-stage world, the stage where it puts on its 'act'. The customer's experience of the moments of truth we mentioned earlier is shaped by everything they perceive in this on-stage world. This is the customers' frame of reference. They don't care about anything off-stage, that's not part of their experience. The product should simply do what it's supposed to do. However, this does not mean that the off-stage world is less important! Anything that goes wrong off-stage, will immediately be noticeable on-stage.

2.5. THE VALUE OF SATISFIED AND LOYAL CUSTOMERS

Customers often unconsciously—and sometimes consciously—compare their experiences with their expectations. If these match, they're simply satisfied. If these exceed their expectations, they're very happy or even excited. If their experiences fall short, they're dissatisfied. This is the outcome of adding up the dissatisfiers, satisfiers and delighters. For the customer, this is the final judgment of all the factors that affect their satisfaction. Satisfaction is a feeling, a snapshot in the wake of a customer service contact or at the end of the customer journey. But it may ultimately determine how satisfied they feel about their whole relationship with your organization.

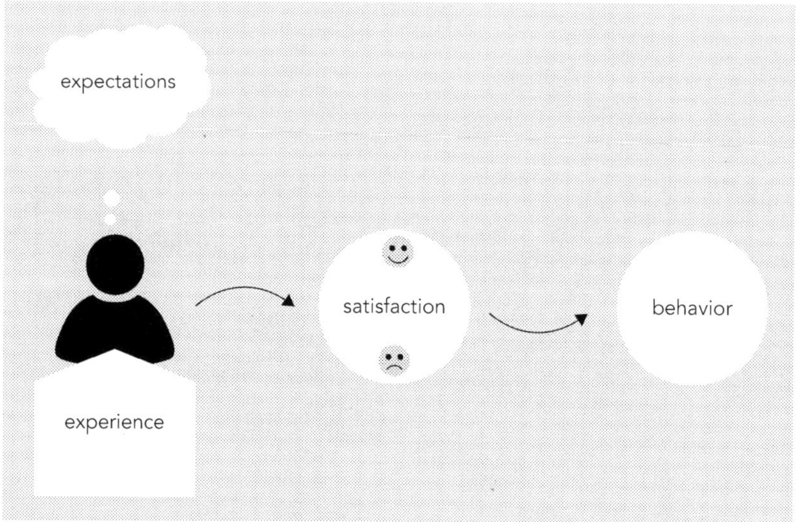

FIGURE 2. What Drives Satisfaction

It goes for demanding customers, too. Their expectations, experiences and satisfaction scores, taken together, determine their behavior. What might be surprising to hear, is that demanding customers can also be turned into loyal customers and great brand ambassadors. They've been known to heap praise, give tips, write positive reviews, and to be cooperative and great to work with. Sound familiar? Customers like that are inspiring. They energize you, unlike nagging, whining, and complaining customers, not to mention the ones who stoop to sabotage and revenge. Various studies show that customers who give your service the highest ratings, from four to five stars, display much more positive behavior than 'generally satisfied' customers. They are three to five times more likely to become return customers.

About 80% to 90% of all recommendations are made by these highly devoted customers.[5] As you can imagine, this doesn't just make you happy, but your whole team and your employer, too. After all, your organization will also see this reflected in their sales figures or other significant metrics.

The Effects of (Dis)Satisfaction

Esteban Kolsky's research[6] shows that 13% (or 1 in every 7 or 8 customers) share their dissatisfaction with 15 people or more. Only 1 in 26 dissatisfied customers tell you, the customer service rep, that they're unhappy.

The number of people who actually make their displeasure known varies depending on the specific study and the year in which it was conducted. According to TARP (Technical Assistance Research Programs - Harvard)[7] 31% of people who experience a problem never tell customer service. These days, complaining is easy, especially on social media.

A truly loyal customer is worth much more than the price of a hotel room, car or plane ticket. Suppose a customer/passenger buys five 500-euro plane tickets per year from the same airline and intends to do so for the next twenty years. This means that—inflation aside—they're likely to spend 20 x 5 x 500 = 50,000 euros. But that's not all. Loyal customers bring in new business by word of mouth. This generates additional sales. At the start of this chapter, we pointed out that customers are the reason you have a job and get paid for it. As you can see, truly happy, loyal customers are a big part of that.

2.6. IN SHORT

Most organizations depend on their customers for survival. Some of those customers are tough, demanding people who are used to World-Class Service, want lots of attention, can act like bullies, or can even be real 'terrors' when they don't get what they expect. Demanding customers usually have higher expectations than 'easy' customers. These expectations are based on your organization's positioning (e.g. high quality, high cost), the customer's previous experiences, the promises your organization has made, what others say about your organization and the customer's own personality. Demanding customers keep raising the bar higher, meaning they're easily dissatisfied and hard to impress. Still, it's possible to turn such demanding customers into loyal, return customers, who act as brand ambassadors for your organization.

REALITY CHECK

- What percentage of the customers you deal with would you describe as demanding customers?
- How do they behave?
- How high are their expectations?
- How do their expectations differ from those of 'easy' customers'?
- What – to them – are dissatisfiers, satisfiers and delighters?
- In what ways are demanding customers valuable to your organization?

READ MORE

Moments of Truth
Jan Carlzon – ISBN 9780060915803

Moments of Magic
Shep Hyken – ISBN 9780963782021

3 WHY ORGANIZATIONS FOCUS ON WORLD-CLASS SERVICE

3.1. INTRODUCTION

In the previous chapter, we showed you that it's not enough to just satisfy your customers. Satisfied is a good starting point, but actually you should see the relationship between an organization and its customers as a marriage. As sales training guru Jeffrey Gitomer[8] once asked: 'Do you want your spouse to be satisfied, or do you want your spouse to be loyal?'

It's all about your customers' expectations, experience and satisfaction. This determines whether they'll recommend you or your organization, and return to buy your organization's products and services again. More and more managers and board members are catching on to this.

This chapter discusses how top and mid-level management are making the customer journey the focus of their organization-wide strategy. This will help you understand where they're coming from and why they make certain choices. We'll first discuss the strategic choices they make, and then we'll deal with what implications this has for the organization. Lastly, we'll look at how these choices are executed. Organizations that aspire to deliver World-Class Service, even for demanding customers, invest in making sure every customer has a great experience all around.

3.2. YOUR ORGANIZATION'S STRATEGIC CHOICES

Many managers and CEOs will recall learning in school that there are three value strategies[9] they can choose from: Operational Excellence, Product Leadership or Customer Intimacy. A value strategy is a choice that sets the course for what the organization aims to be best at and becomes the touchstone for every corporate decision. Below, we'll briefly explain the three strategies.

The Operational Excellence strategy was originally aimed at increasing customer value while also reducing cost. Unfortunately, many organizations seem to have forgotten about the first part of this equation and use it as a cost reduction tool only, without considering whether this is good or bad for their customers. Boards particularly tend to opt for this strategy when times are tough: no spending is allowed, efficiency is key, everything has to be digitalized, there's no room for catering to individual customers. Austerity is paramount. The priority is cutting costs, often at the expense of customer service and customer experience. Programs with grand names like 'Thrift to Thrive' and 'Do More with Less' lead to layoffs, digitalization of services, shorter business hours and doing away with any type of personalization.

The Product Leadership strategy is all about creating the best possible products: the hottest, technically most advanced, most user-friendly or best designed items. Businesses like Apple and Tesla rely heavily on this strategy. In such product-driven organizations it's all about innovation, quality and perfection. These organizations either target innovators and early adopters[10], who are happy to try out new and innovative products, or consumers who are passionate about one particular aspect of life (e.g. the environment). Customer value is seldom a leading rule for them; they care about innovation.

Organizations that choose to go with Customer Intimacy as their strategy strive to build up a close relationship with their customers. They try to achieve this by knowing their customers, fully catering to their needs and expectations, putting customer experience first, and offering tailored services. In this competitive strategy, organizations prioritize the customer in everything they do.

The problem with value strategies is that an organization's focus can shift depending on company performance and the kind of mandate management gets from the board. This can cause a yo-yo strategy that's all about cost cutting one year, and customer experience the next. The bosses can appear unable to set a steady course. But it doesn't have to be that way. Successful businesses like Singapore Airlines use a combination of value creation strategies. For them, it's not either/or, but both. They do the seemingly impossible; they are one of the most efficient airlines in the world, and one of the most customer-oriented at the same time. This is how they achieve this: Every business unit that involves customer contact (the 'on-stage' world), such as check in and in-flight service, take a Customer Intimacy strategy. The back office, the 'off-stage' world that the customer never sees, is run on an Operational Excellence basis. This dual strategy is also known as ambidexterity (being both left and right-handed and equally good with both).

3.3. WORLD-CLASS SERVICE, EVEN FOR DEMANDING CUSTOMERS

You might work for an organization that has opted for Customer Intimacy as its competitive strategy. That might mean you're familiar with concepts such as Service Excellence, Customer Excellence, customer-oriented, customer- centricity or World-Class Service. In this setting, service does not refer to the freebees you offer your customers, but the total service experience. It's 'taking action to add value for the customer'. In the services industry, this includes anything and everything you do for your customers. In the products industry, this includes all the support, maintenance, help and advice you provide your customers with.

In certain lines of business, such as five-star hotels, luxury cars, exclusive salons and yacht building, offering World-Class Service to demanding customers is routine. Many customers in these segments expect only the very best. If you don't offer them World-Class Service, you're bound to lose their business. But even in less high-end industries, the number of demanding customers is on the rise. If you fail to meet their expectations, you'll end up losing some of them too.

By the way, there's no good reason why public and not-for-profit organizations such as city hall, low-rent housing corporations and care facilities should not offer great service to their demanding customers as well. After all, these customers often have nowhere else to turn. So, public organizations are morally obliged to help them to the best of their ability. And these customers can teach organizations a lot. Demanding customers are often the vanguard of a much larger group of customers who – over time – will develop the same expectations. And let's be honest, in some cases, customers are called 'demanding' while actually their expectations are not so over the top. For instance, government institutions are legally required to respond to a complaint within six weeks, but people are right to wonder why it has to take so long.

As we wrote in our preface, this book is not about letting your customers walk all over you. Some customers go too far, become aggressive or blackmail a business with bad reviews if they're not given a free night's stay. Obviously, that's beyond the pale. Even World-Class Service to demanding customers has its limits.

3.4. WORKING ON WORLD-CLASS SERVICE

Service is only top-tier if your customers experience it as such. In short, your service has to be excellent. The best your customers have experienced. Any organization that aspires to this, takes a variety of measures to create the desired result. It's about creating a total experience, in which anything and everything your customers perceive matters. To determine their service policy, organizations first define the ideal customer experience. How do they want their customers to perceive the organization? Fast? Close? Personal? Pro-active? Amazing? A particular mix of these values? Based on the answer to this question, management does what is necessary to consistently create this ideal experience every day, in every customer service moment. The measures they take to create this experience are at the level of People & Culture, Hardware, Customer Journeys & Organization and Communications.

> *Excellent service doesn't just happen. It's the result of high ambition, true effort, intelligent direction, skilled execution and the ability to see obstacles as opportunities*

For **People & Culture**, some measures could be: recruiting and hiring truly customer-oriented representatives, putting the customer first even during the on-boarding period, offering skills training and coaching, staffing heavily enough to enable representatives to provide good service, and emphasizing top-tier service in internal communication.

Hardware measures have to do with the physical objects your customers come into contact with, as well as all the means that your organization uses to create an excellent customer experience. This ranges from the layout and decoration of a physical space, to the look and feel of your website, to the coffee cups you use.

Customer Journeys & Organization measures are about arranging the processes and physical objects your customers encounter in order to make their experience ideal. Any customer journey consists of several stages. When going out to eat, for example, it consists of: visiting a website, making a reservation, finding the restaurant and parking the car, being welcomed upon arrival, hanging up coats, getting into the elevator (see Fig. 3) as well as the next stages of being shown to the table, ordering an aperitif, studying the menu, ordering the food, waiting for the food, eating the food, going to the restroom, paying the check, getting the coats and leaving the building.

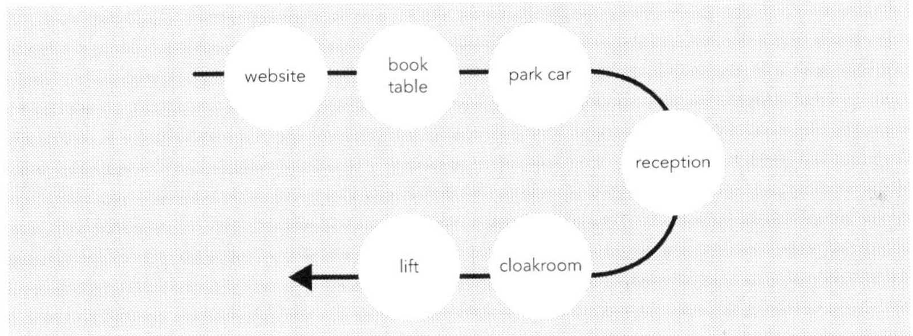

FIGURE 3. Sample Customer Journey

Each of these stages should contribute to an ideal customer experience. If your organization wants to be perceived as fast, for instance, it will take measures to speed up the pace of service. Changing the organizational structure can help achieve this. For example, if uncooperativeness between departments slows down service, it helps to set up customer service teams in which people from different departments work together to create a great customer experience. Such teams actually become mini enterprises with their own customer base. Customer service representatives also play an important role. Wherever you work, as a customer service rep you play a major part in reinforcing the customer experience. Your actions directly affect the customer. Remember that in the 'customer experience chain' the ultimate experience is only as good as its weakest link.

Communications measures are aimed at the image your organization wants to project to its customers. What texts and images does your organization use? What promises does it make to its customers? Clearly, the message should fit the ideal customer experience.

All these measures are intended to ensure that your customers' experiences match the ideal experience. Such measures were part and parcel of the original design of Disney amusement parks and they are still the basis of Disney's daily park operations. A growing number of organizations – possibly yours, too – understand this and apply the same rules. That's not a matter of broad strokes, but especially details. For your customers it's precisely the small details that can make the difference between an okay experience and a great one. Too many disruptions in the ideal experience can quickly become irritating. Once the adrenaline levels rise, you're likely to end up with a dissatisfied customer.

3.5. IN SHORT

Organizations tend to use one of three value strategies – Operational Excellence, Product Leadership, Customer Intimacy – to determine what they want to excel in. While quite a few organizations lurch from one value strategy to the next, successful customer-oriented organizations use smart mixes of various strategies. Real customer-oriented organizations set very high standards for themselves. They want all their customers to be happy. Not just the easy ones, but particularly the demanding ones. To this end, they prioritize customer service throughout the whole organization. Such organizations are aware that to consistently offer top-tier service, every organizational unit and department needs to be involved. So they gear their Customer Service Representatives & Culture, Hardware, Customer Journeys & Organization, and Communication towards excellent customer service. Is your organization customer-oriented?

REALITY CHECKS

- What value strategy (or mix of strategies) does your organization use?
- Are customers and offering excellent customer service a priority in your organization?
- Does this apply to demanding customers too?
- What does your organization do to facilitate consistent top-tier service?
- Do your organization's policies on People & Culture, Hardware, Customer Journeys & Organization, and Communication help to create happy customers?

READ MORE

The New Gold Standard: 5 Leadership Principles for Creating a Legendary Customer Experience
Joseph Michelli – ISBN 9780071548335

Delivering Happiness
Tony Hsieh – ISBN 9780446563048

Customer Intimacy: Pick Your Partners, Shape Your Culture, Win Together
Fred Wiersema – ISBN 9781888232004

4 YOU CAN MAKE A DIFFERENCE

4.1. INTRODUCTION

The previous chapter focused on the ambitions of managers and CEOs. Sure, what they want to achieve is important. But they won't get anywhere without people like you, the employee who is in direct contact with the customer. Only you can exceed customers' expectations, put the customer – even the demanding customer – first, and turn them into loyal brand ambassadors.
An organization can only live up to its goal of offering World-Class Service by providing great service every day, to each and every customer. You are the key to the organization's success. This chapter focuses on what that means.

4.2. PEOPLE MAKE A DIFFERENCE

Your attitude towards others determines their attitude towards you.

Research shows that it's people who make the difference between poor, fair and great service. That's why so many organizations in the services industry still prioritize personal contact with a sales rep, call center rep, service engineer or other role first.

What this means is that your attitude and actions, often about the smallest issues, are crucial. The personal touch is essential to get 5-star ratings. Various studies have shown that customer satisfaction following in-person contact or a personal phone call is much higher than after written or digital contact.

A survey of private bank clients revealed that interactions with the account manager were crucial. This person could make or break the customer's relationship with the bank. Several independent studies confirm these findings. A study into shoppers' delight[11] (what makes shoppers happy?) concluded that salespeople are the main reason customers rave about a store. The Top 5 reasons for customers to rate a store very highly include salespeople's extreme helpfulness, friendliness, solution-oriented mindset, not being too pushy and taking the time to help them.

A Michelin-star Spanish restaurant offers shipshape basic service: the table linen is crisp, the glasses polished, the food top-notch and the wines delicious. But what makes the difference is the restaurant's personal touch. The chef/owner is there every night and frequently strolls into the dining room. He can get upset at a wrong place setting and obsesses about every little detail. Perfection is about dedication and eye for detail. This man has surgical precision when it comes to details. His customers are everything to him. He loves them. He talks to them, not too often and not too long, but just long enough for it to be experienced as pleasant.

4.3 THE SIX RULES

When you are a customer, do you ever get the sense that the service rep you're talking to has just had a refresher course? Does it feel like someone is going through the motions? An artificial approach does not feel sincere. If a waiter asks you whether you're enjoying your holiday, but doesn't seem interested in the answer, why do they even ask? Because they were told to? Because it's the norm? Demanding customers know immediately whether your actions as a service rep are sincere or not. They want tailor-made service and they don't care about rules and procedures. Like we said, you – and your actions and attitude – can make all the difference in your customer contact. But what you do must be real and come from your heart. Your actions shouldn't just be based on rules and procedures. They should be inspired by how you think customers deserve to be treated. They should be inspired by how you <u>are</u>. Sincere, spontaneous, authentic, real and genuine.

Based on research and our personal experience with organizations, we have come up with six rules for exceptional customer experience. These rules are meant for customer service representatives who deal with demanding customers. The rules are not checklists or procedures, but rather guidelines for you to keep in mind in your day-to-day dealings with customers. They can help you make the right choices.

Figure 4 shows where these rules fit into the customer satisfaction meter. The number range on the left (1-10) is the level of customer satisfaction. These correspond to three experience levels[12]. At the lowest level – Basics covered – customer expectations are met. Customers feel welcome and at the most basic level, everything is taken care of. We've included 'Feeling welcome' at the lowest

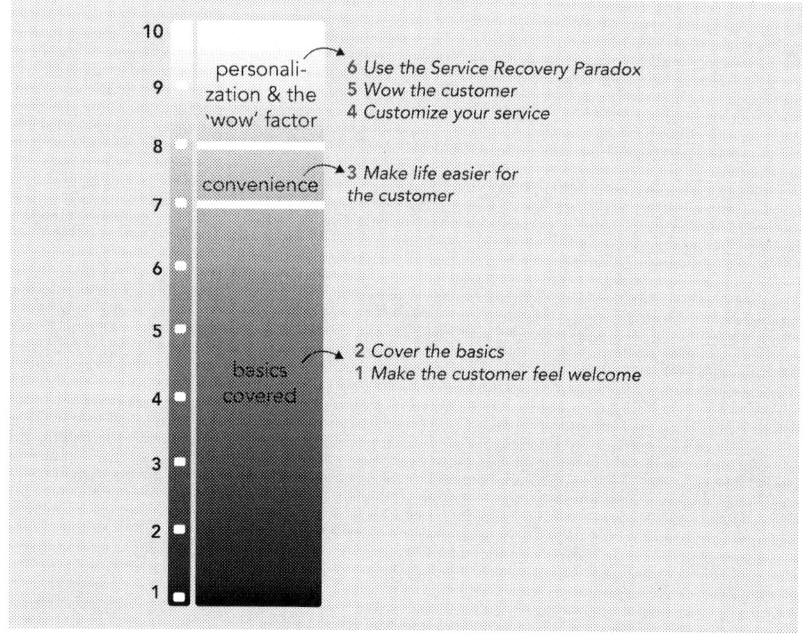

FIGURE 4. Where the Six Rules Fit into the Three Experience Levels

level because many customers, and most definitely demanding customers, consider this part of a basic service level.

In fact, anything in this category is a dissatisfier. If you only meet these expectations, customers will rate your service 7 max.

1. *Make the customer feel welcome*
   Always give customers a warm welcome, because first impressions tend to set the tone and determine their behavior to a large extent. Hospitality remains key during your customers' entire encounter with your organization. Make sure they keep feeling welcome at every stage of their customer journey. Customers are not inconvenient interruptions of your job, they <u>are</u> <u>the essence</u> of your job!

2. *Cover the basics*
Make sure that the basics customers expect are in order: honor your agreements, look well-groomed, know your job, be efficient, and so on. This is how you prevent customer dissatisfaction. In addition, you only do things that you can explain to your customers and that they can understand, so you can continue to look them in the eye. The basics are mostly things that you would also consider minimum requirements if you were the customer.

The middle level is 'Convenience'. The rule that corresponds to this level is 'Make life easier'. Let your customers know you are making things easy for them. Take on the work, and most importantly, the mental burden. If you can make your customers feel they're in good hands, and the basics are in order too, they'll usually give your service an 8 out of 10.

3. *Make life easier for the customer*
Make sure your customers don't have to do anything unnecessary. Don't make them do anything that you can take off their hands by being proactive. Make life as easy as possible for them. Apply the KISS motto: Keep It Short and Simple.

The highest experience level is Personalization and The Wow Factor. This is the level where you can really make a difference for demanding customers. Three rules apply here. 'Customizing your service to the customer' is the way to let your customers feel how important they are. This is one of the most important ways to turn them into fans that give you a 9 or even a 10 out of 10. The other two rules are 'Wow the customer' and 'Use the Service Recovery Paradox'. These rules are all about outdoing yourself, providing service that exceeds their expectations.

4. Customize your service

Offer your customers tailored service; it makes them feel appreciated. It gives them a sense of warmth, attention and of being taken seriously. Knowing your customers and catering to their individual needs and preferences makes them feel recognized and valued.

5. Wow the customer

Develop your instincts for situations where you can positively wow your customers by exceeding their expectations. Take time to provide little acts of kindness—or big acts if appropriate—to make your customers go 'wow!' Remember the Ritz Carlton and Joshie the Giraffe.[13]

6. Use the Service Recovery Paradox

Happily tackle any problems and complaints. Put in the extra work to solve them, even if neither you personally nor your organization is to blame. You know you can make a difference, so you cut the endless back and forth and just solve the problem!

> *We are what we repeatedly do. Excellence, then, is not an act, but a habit*
>
> **ARISTOTELES**

The next six chapters will discuss these six rules of excellent customer service in more detail. They are intended to help you understand exactly what we mean, what your strong points are, and where there's room for improvement. They will give you pointers that you can immediately put into practice on the job. You can also discuss them with your whole team or department so you can work on them together. But first we'd like to ask you to take a good look at yourself. What makes you tick? What drives the way you act towards customers? What do you love about your job? These are hard questions, but it pays to stop and think about them before we explore the six rules in greater depth.

4.4. WHAT MAKES YOU TICK?

Let's take a three-step approach that will help you to look at yourself. We'll start by asking how customers see you. How do they experience your service? How do they rate it? Then we'll ask you to look at your own personality traits. What type of person are you? For example, are you more of an introvert or an extravert? And finally, we'll ask you to find what intrinsically motivates you. Note that we're not talking about deep psychological insights and personality tests. If you feel the need for those, ask your employer.

Step 1: How do your customers rate you?
A recent study of more than 25 interactions between a utility company's call center and its customers found that, under the same conditions, customers gave individual call center reps ratings ranging from 6 to 9. As it turned out, under the same conditions, customer satisfaction with individual reps ranged from 6 to 9 based on 25+ interactions. Clearly, a customer service representative can make a difference. So, how do your customers rate your service? And if you asked the customers you helped what impression you made on them, what would they say? Look at the table below and

check one of the four boxes between the two statements. Are your scores clustered on the left or on the right side?

This...	Very	A little	A little	Very	Or this...?
Eager to learn new things every day					I like routines, every day is more or less the same
Enthusiastic					Indifferent
Smiling					Serious – emotionless (or even grumpy)
Friendly					Cool – distant
Committed					Non-committal
Interested					Not interested
Tailored service					Process oriented
Spare no effort					Everything's an effort
The glass is half full					The glass is half empty
Leave it to me, I'll handle that					That's not my job
I'll look into that for you					If it's not there, it's not in stock
Flexible					Red tape
Available					9 to 5 (minus breaks)
Yes, unless					No, unless
Spontaneous					Stick to procedures
Connect with the customer					Just doing a job
Follow me please					Aisle 3, back there, near the freezers

FIGURE 5. Your Profile

Step 2: Your personality

You can also take things a step further and take a closer look at your own personality. What kind of person are you? There are many models than can help you figure this out. One of them is Jung's personality model.[14] Psychologist Carl Jung distinguished eight different personality types, four of which fall into the category 'extraverted' and four into 'introverted.' Are you mainly extraverted or introverted? What subtype are you?

Extraverted (high-energy, excited, assertive)	Introverted (aloof, quiet, level-headed)
The thinking type	The thinking type
The feeling type	The feeling type
The sensing type	The sensing type
The intuitive type	The intuitive type

FIGURE 6. Jung's Eight Different Personality Types

Your personality type influences your behavior. So, it's important to get an idea of what kind of person you are. There are several tests based on Jung's personality model. You should take one, such as the Big Five personality test[15]. It uses five dimensions to help you understand your own personality. Figure 7 shows these dimensions and what your score on them means.[16]
There are many other options available online, including Jung's test and variations of the Big Five test. We highly recommend that you try one or more to discover more about yourself.

Step 3: Your intrinsic motivation
What drives you? What puts pep in your step at work? Professional athletes love their sport and want to win. What do you love about your job? What brings you joy? What fires you up? You can probably imagine that people who like interacting and communicating with people approach their job differently than those who don't care about that.

	High scores	Low scores
1. **Openness:** the extent to which you're open to or curious about new experiences	– You're intellectually curious – You're open to new experiences	– You dislike risks – You prefer to avoid uncertainties – You distrust different ideas – You're predictable – You stay in your comfort zone
2. **Conscien-tiousness:** how aware you are of your actions and their consequences	– You're organized – You're reliable – You're determined – You're ambitious – You set high personal goals – You're goal-oriented – You manage your time well	– You're less motivated – You're chaotic and less well-organized – You're not always on time – You have a carefree lifestyle – You act on impulses
3. **Extraversion:** whether you need a lot of social contact or not	– You like to meet new people – You find it easy to introduce yourself to strangers – You're energetic – You're social – You're talkative – You like big groups of people – You're constantly seeking attention	– You're reserved – You're shy and subdued – You get energy from your inner experiences – You're not so talkative – You feel intimidated in big groups of people – You prefer smaller groups
4. **Altruism:** an attitude or belief in which you base your actions on what is good for others	– You're friendly – You're helpful – You're trusting – You're accommodating – You put a lot of trust in others – You're always ready to lend a hand – You value working together – You don't like confrontations and conflicts – You like doing others a favor	– You're a know-it-all – You're competitive – You're not terribly helpful – You're not very accommodating – You distrust other people's intentions – You're selfish – You seek your own advantage
5. **Neuroticism:** the extent to which you appear either sensitive and nervous or self-assured and carefree	– You're emotionally stable – You tend not to worry – You have positive self-image – You stay calm in stressful situations – You see problems for what they are	– You're irritable – You tend to feel restless – You tend to have emotional outbursts – You often sweat the small stuff – You often focus on problems – You make problems bigger than they are

FIGURE 7. The Big Five Personality Test

Demanding customers have high expectations. So you'll have to set aside your personal pride a bit, assume that their remarks aren't meant personally, find creative solutions, and be on your toes, day in and day out. Do you see this as a burden or as a welcome challenge? If you consider it a welcome challenge, you're probably highly motivated to go to work every day. Are you?

4.5. WHAT DEMANDS DOES THIS PLACE ON YOU?

Obviously, things are easier if the conditions you work in allow you to put your customers front and center. That's up to your boss and your management (see Chapter 11). Either way, you play a crucial role. Because you're a real-life person, you can make a big difference in how your customers experience your organization's service. Your personal effort, commitment, drive, and willingness to learn largely determine how well you perform your role. When a customer calls or appears at the desk, you are the public face of your organization. Not management, not the shareholders, not your boss, but YOU! The face the customer sees, and the voice the customer hears, is your own. But it's also the organization's. What demands does this place on you? To answer this question, we will introduce four key concepts: 1. Chopped liver 2. Eye for detail 3. Teamwork and 4. Continuous improvement.

Chopped liver

Maybe you sell a car or a house every day, talk to dozens of customers on the phone, serve hundreds of passengers on a plane, or help dozens of guests check into your hotel. It's all routine to you, but for your customers it might be a special moment. Perhaps the customer who's buying that car or motorbike had to save up for years to afford it, or the person on the other end of the line has a serious medical problem. Maybe the person who sent you that email has just suffered a great loss. These customers don't deserve to be treated like chopped liver, as the saying goes. So this requires you to regard every customer as unique, to offer them great, personal service, every single day. What it comes down to is attitude, which is defined by Merriam Webster's dictionary as a feeling or way of thinking that affects a person's behavior. So, in customer service, your attitude should always be positive! As Earl Nightingale[17] said in his 1957 recorded speech *The Strangest Secret*: "You become what you think about."

Eye for Detail

Little things can make a world of difference. Silverware should be placed with surgical precision next to the perfectly placed flatware, making every place setting identical. A glass should be served with the drink's brand logo facing the customer. The cashier should get up from behind the register to hand over the shopping bag full of purchases, with the handle positioned exactly so the customer can easily grab it. There are so many more examples: a flawless letter, a handwritten note left on the night table in a hotel room, a kind, personal comment during a phone conversation.

Most of these minute details cost absolutely nothing, but they make a huge difference in how your customers experience your service. An eye for detail sometimes requires an almost obsessive eye for perfection. You have to be on the lookout for the smallest gesture that might please your customers. When everyone has mastered this art, an organization's customer experience becomes extraordinary. When your customers start to notice that you've thought of everything (even the unexpected), you've entered the realm of wow factors.

Teamwork

A chain is only as strong as its weakest link. In many cases, offering World-Class Service is a team effort. To offer your customers great service, you have to rely not only your own competencies, but also those of your co-workers or teammates. That's why it's important that you show team spirit and a willingness to contribute to the joint effort. It's 'not everyone for themself,' but 'one for all and all for one.' Winning is something you do as a team. Therefore, it's important that you and all your team members:

- share the same (service) goals;
- know and appreciate each other;
- are enthusiastic about the job;
- train together;
- combine forces and coordinate efforts;
- take ownership of the same service-oriented culture;
- communicate well;
- know you can rely on each other.

As a team, you should operate like clockwork and help each other to offer your customers World-Class Service. You need to have a handle on your own work (see Fig. 8, circle of control). And, you should have some influence on your team (circle of influence). However, there are probably other teams or departments that are further away, yet you still rely on them sometimes in your quest to help your customers (circle of concern).

They might be further away, but don't hesitate to try to influence them too! After all, you're the public face of your organization and if you need their help, it's important to be able to count on them.

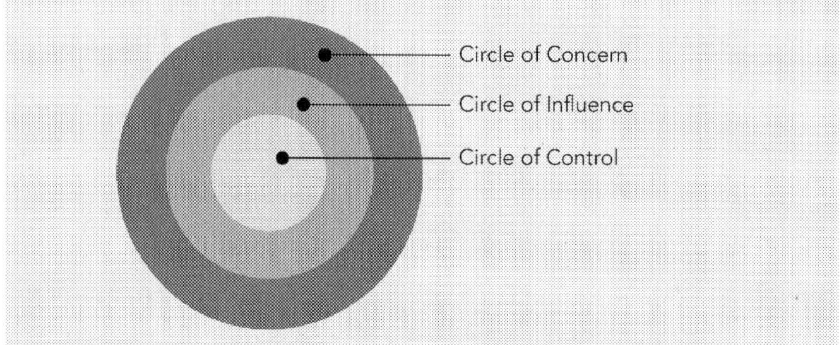

FIGURE 8. The Circles of Control, Influence and Concern

Continuous Improvement

Professional athletes train every day. This is how they get better at what they do. Nobody is perfect. There's always something new to learn or old to improve. Be aware of this and apply the Plan-Do-Check-Act (PDCA) rule. This means that you regularly check the quality of your work. How do your customers and co-workers experience your performance? What's going well and what could you improve? What can you do differently? Your basic attitude is that you're eager to learn. Maybe you think: 'I've worked at this job for twenty years, what could I possibly still need to learn?' Well, we've got news for you in particular: there's always room for improvement. That's why you should love getting feedback. Sure, it feels great to get compliments and pats on the back, but constructive criticism about things you could do better is more valuable. Therefore, you should regularly attend training sessions to gain new insights and expand your skill set. That's how you remain that professional athlete who performs at the top of their league, offering World-Class Service to demanding customers.

Today I will do what others won't so tomorrow I can do what others can't.

JERRY RICE

4.6. IN SHORT

As a customer service representative, you are the factor that makes the difference between adequate, good and World-Class Service. How do your customers rate you? What are your personality traits and how do these influence how you act towards your customers? You could be introverted, or extraverted, with four possible subtypes (thinking, feeling, sensing and intuitive). Your motivation also plays an important role. What do you love about your job? What motivates you to get out of bed every morning? Do you see demanding customers as a burden or a welcome challenge? Offering great service to demanding customers is like being a professional athlete. It requires a lot of dedication. You have to avoid getting into a rut and treating your customers like chopped liver. You need to have an eye for detail, be a good team player and continually raise your game. Remember, you can make a difference. And, as the old Chinese proverb has it: 'To serve is to rule!'

REALITY CHECKS

- How do you make a difference for your customers?
- How do your customers rate you? Is this score – your current performance – the best you can do?
- What are your personality traits?
- What motivates you in your work? What do you love about your job?
- Do you see demanding customers as a welcome challenge?

READ MORE

The Strangest Secret
Earl Nightingale - ISBN 9781603865579

You Can If You Think You Can
Norman Vincent Peale - ISBN 9780671765910

Think and Grow Rich
Napoleon Hill - ISBN 9781585424337

Just Looking Thanks!
Alf Dunbar - ISBN 9781412094139

The Essentials of Business Etiquette
Barbara Pachter - ISBN 9780071811262

Insanely Great Customer Service
Daniella Fairbairn - ISBN 9781523473618

7 Habits of Highly Effective People
Stephen R. Covey - ISBN 978198213727

PART B

THE SIX RULES OF CREATING EXCEPTIONAL CUSTOMER EXPERIENCES

5 MAKE THE CUSTOMER FEEL WELCOME

5.1. INTRODUCTION

The first blow is half the battle. First encounters and first impressions, and sometimes even the moments leading up to these, can influence how your customers experience everything that follows. This is all the more true of demanding customers. Which is why we're going to tackle this rule first. It starts even before your encounter with your customer begins. If the customer journey has worked flawlessly so far, you're off to a great start. But sometimes, your customer already has some negative baggage by the time you first speak to them because of some hiccup during an earlier part of the customer journey. If things have gone less than perfect so far, your customer might already be in a bad mood. Next, we want to impress upon you the importance of knowing and acknowledging your customers, of giving them a warm reception and finding a way to click with them. These are key elements in the art of making them feel welcome. We'll discuss these elements one by one in the paragraphs ahead. Don't forget: you can only make a first impression once, so make sure it's excellent. It should almost be like love at first sight. Figure 9 shows the four elements of this first rule.

FIGURE 9. The Four Elements of Rule 1, Make Customers Feel Welcome

5.2. BEFORE THE FIRST ENCOUNTER: BAD BAGGAGE

An eye clinic in a large city found a way to offer its patients a trouble-free customer journey before actual treatment. Surveys had revealed that getting to the hospital and parking in particular gave patients worries and stress. The clinic responded by introducing a valet service. So you see, making someone feel welcome starts well before the first face-to-face encounter, at an earlier stage of the customer journey. This is relevant whether you're going to meet a customer, setting up a digital meeting, or the customer is coming over to meet you. It doesn't matter whether that meeting takes place at your office, your store, your hotel or anywhere else: the easier it is for the customer to get there, the more welcome they feel. The convenience you create at this stage also sets the mood for your meeting. This is particularly relevant when it's the customer's first time visiting your location, when that location is not so easy to find, or when parking is a

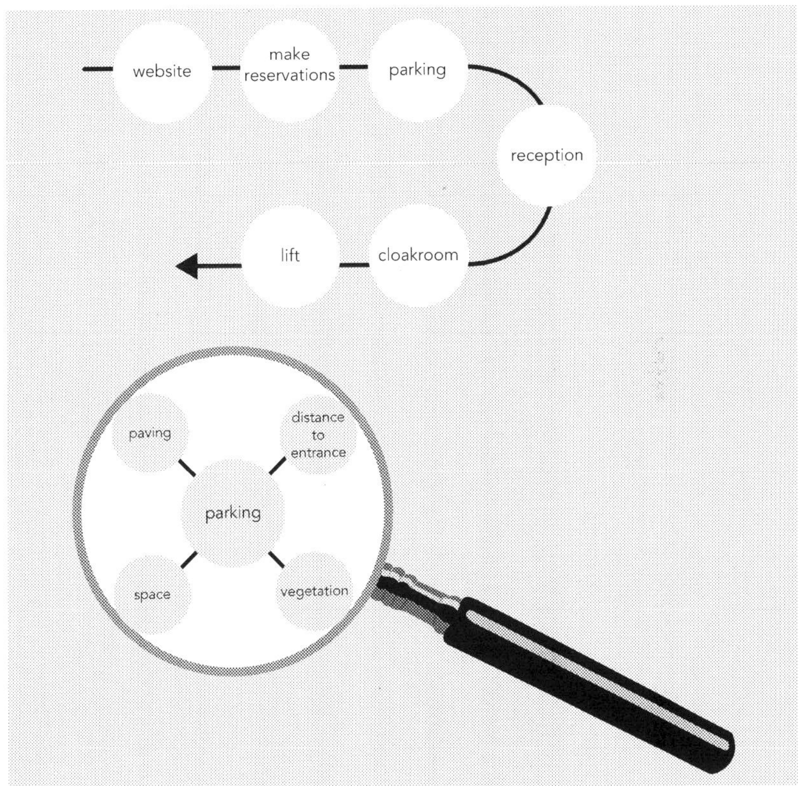

FIGURE 10. Zooming in on parking as part of the customer journey

problem. If you neglect this part of the journey, your customer could arrive stressed and angry to your first encounter. To prevent this, send your customers personalized directions beforehand, complete with suggestions for parking and warnings about possible obstacles. If your organization has its own parking lot or garage, reserve a space and notify the customer ("Welcome, Ms Johnson - Widget Industries"). If you think none of this is going to work, arrange for them to be picked up at their door. If they're late, arrange for someone to park their car so they can jump out and walk in. Such pro-active service is, of course, not reserved for customers who arrive by car. You can also make things as easy as possible for customers who rely on public transportation. It's all about making your customers feel welcome.

1. **Prevent stress prior to the meeting**
2. **Keep in mind that customers may have some 'baggage' based on earlier experiences**

The following example shows how important it is to be prepared for customers with negative baggage. A large group of tourists who had booked a vacation in a tropical Club Med resort ran into all sorts of problems on the way there. Due to delays and other problems, the group was going to arrive at the airport in the middle of the night. The resort manager could see this coming and understood that if he did nothing, his guests would be in a foul mood by the time they arrived at the resort. He realized he needed to act, even though none of this was his fault. So he got his staff to welcome the guests with cocktails, food and music in the airport's arrival hall. The guests loved it! Despite the stress they'd already been through, they felt their exceptionally warm welcome set the tone for the rest of their stay.

So be prepared for baggage. Sometimes, when a customer shows up at your desk, they're already upset, angry or downright unreasonable. These are the real demanding customers who test your professionalism. Their previous flight may have been late or your organization may have failed to deliver crucial products on time. Maybe there's been an unpleasant exchange between the customer and one of your co-workers. It could be anything.

So you might think: 'What did I do to deserve this?' Nine times out of ten, it has absolutely nothing to do with you. Customers are not angry or disappointed with you, but with whatever happened earlier on.

It's not your fault, so don't take it personally. It's not a reflection on you, but on your organization, or even an entirely different organization. Be prepared for such 'baggage' and see it as a welcome challenge to turn this disgruntled customer back into a happy customer.
Keep in mind that, even though it's not your fault, your organization still depends on you to take responsibility. You are still the organization's public face. So stay professional, always maintain the moral high ground and never let your emotions take over, however difficult this may be. Ranting customers tend to feel helpless and fear that your organization won't take their problem seriously anyway. Prove them wrong and treat them like royalty.

5.3. KNOW AND ACKNOWLEDGE YOUR CUSTOMERS

First impressions are hugely important. A customer's first impression colors the rest of their experience and actions. There's always a first time the customer calls, boards the plane, takes a seat at the hotel bar, gets a visit from the realtor or meets their lawyer. The first four minutes of a face-to-face encounter, and the first 20 to 60 seconds of a phone call set the tone for the rest of the encounter[16] and maybe even the rest of the customer journey. Customers unwittingly make use of the halo rule here. If their first impression is positive, they'll notice other positive events more. If their first impression is negative, then subsequent negative events will stand out more. You understand the mechanism, right?

Experience and emotions reinforce each other. That's why the first impression is so important.

Next time you board a plane, note how the cabin crew welcome you, look you in the eye, give you friendly and sincere smiles, and wish you a good flight. Also note how this makes you feel. It's free, but being seen and being made to feel welcome are hugely important. As a customer service rep you can offer your customers the same feeling, even if you're not a cabin crew member. Noticing someone, a friendly nod, eye contact and a welcoming attitude are often all it takes.

1. **The first impression often determines the whole experience**
2. **Let your customer know you've seen them first; making eye contact is often sufficient**
3. **Recognize your customers, address them by name**
4. **Be careful, customers can sense what you think of them**

In many cases, it's not too hard to notice and acknowledge your customers. But what if you're very busy? What if there's a line of customers at your reception desk, or you're helping another customer? What if you have to combine helping customers with other types of work? Your office might be understaffed, or your workload heavy. That complicates matters. But giving a customer the feeling that you've noticed them still has to be your priority. A nod and eye contact are often all it takes. If your busy with all sorts of administrative tasks while the line of customers is growing, you need to realize that waiting customers usually don't understand why you don't drop everything to help them. They wonder "Does this person not see me? It's crazy that I have to wait so long!" So, either help this customer immediately, or do your administrative work in the back, out of sight. Demanding customers are often pressed for time and hate waiting. You should therefore use anything at your disposal to reduce or at least cushion their waiting time. Your organization can take action by having extra staff on call – "Jonah, please report to checkout lane 6, Jonah, lane 6" – or by installing a button under the reception desk that you can use to call in your manager's help when the line gets too long or you're having problems.

As a hospitality business you should not tell your customers about your hospitality, you should show them, according to Dutch 5-star hotelier Camille Oostwegel. Hospitality is more than being friendly and attentive, it's also being considerate with your environment, the buildings and nature. It's much more than putting a gold tap in the bathroom. Just like the essence of feeling welcome – knowing you're really received with open arms – is much more than stepping onto a welcome mat. Hospitality, a warm welcome, and a good atmosphere are all part of a warm feeling you convey to your guests. Hospitality is not just what you do. It's who you *are*.

Recognizing your customers is important too. There's a world of difference between "Good morning, Mr. Peters, I'll be right with you" and "Good morning, sir." Whenever possible, make sure you recognize a return customer and refer to them by name. This is particularly important when your customer is aware that you should know them, like when they've been there before. In some cases, it can even be appropriate to refer to customers by name on their first visit. Take for instance a high-end law firm. Only four to five clients per day will come in and reception knows exactly when they're expected. The receptionists googles the visitors and finds their pictures and a few details. This allows them to address the client by name as they enter, and it integrates recognition into their reception.

First impressions are also affected by the interplay between the impression you make on the customer and the impression they make on you. This can be positive, but it can also be a negative spiral. If your first impression of the customer is bad because he's rude or impatient, or looks unkempt, the customer will notice what you think. No matter how you act, they will know. That will have a negative influence on them, and a negative spiral is born. In short, always try to put yourself in the customer's shoes and think positively of them.

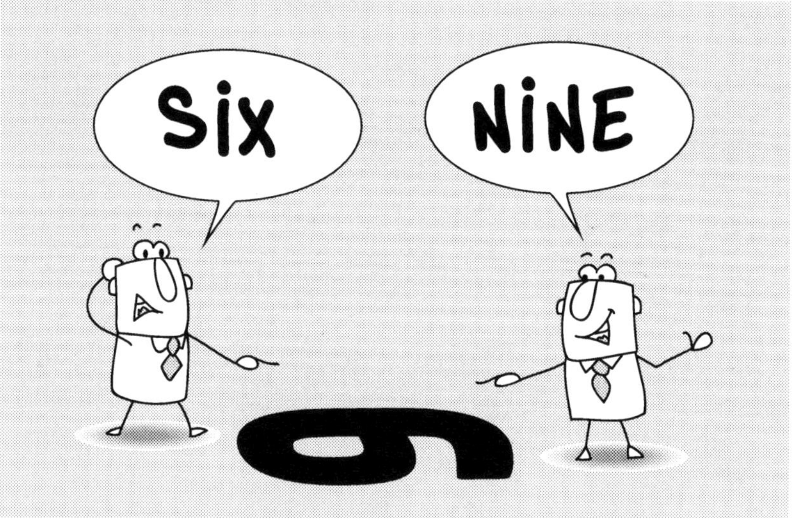

FIGURE 11. It's often a matter of perception and point of view

10-Foot Rule
Many years ago, Walmart decided that any customer who comes within a 10-foot range of an employee, should be met with a smile, eye contact, a warm greeting and an offer of help.

5.4. ROLL OUT THE RED CARPET: A WARM WELCOME

What we mean by the red carpet treatment is best illustrated by a new policy introduced by a car dealership. As soon as a customer parks their car, the receptionist leaves the desk and walks over to the entrance to personally welcome the customer. From there, the receptionist accompanies the customer to the employee they need to see. This is a warm welcome; the receptionist rolls out a red carpet, so to speak. And if it it's raining, the receptionist goes further. They grab an umbrella and meet the customer at their parked car, to make sure they stay dry on the way in.

The French use the word *l'accueil* for the way in which people are welcomed. This word means something more than just welcome. It has a built-in spirit of warmth and generosity that describes exactly what we mean by 'warm welcome'. Customers should be made to feel truly welcome, pampered even. This is just as valid for customers calling on the phone or chatting with you online, as it is for face-to-face encounters. Customers should feel that you consider them important and that you're happy to help.

"Welcome to Changi Airport in Singapore." Whatever country you fly to, you're asked to show your passport upon arrival. Customs officers are usually not able to welcome you in your own language. Most travelers will understand the words "Passport please", but Changi Airport wanted to be friendlier. So their officials give travelers a friendly nod and stretch out their hand to take the passport. After the standard passport check, they hand it back with a smile, a nod and a gesture toward a bowl of individually wrapped peppermints. Without actually saying anything, these officials are welcoming you to Singapore. A warm welcome in the shape of a friendly gesture and a nod.

1. **Give your customers the red carpet treatment**
2. **Give them a sincere, nice, genuine welcome**
3. **Show some emotion in your welcome, focusing on them instead of what you are doing**
4. **Take your time for each customer**
5. **Write a personal note to them**
6. **Make customers feel welcome even when they leave**

Never leave a customer waiting when they arrive – not even when they're early. And don't make them feel guilty if they're late. Welcome them with a friendly smile and a heartfelt greeting. Just like a skilled maître d' in a Michelin star restaurant, it's your job to welcome, help, pamper and thank your customers. They want to be helped right away. They don't literally need a red carpet, but they do want to enter through a clean, tidy entrance, possibly decorated with a vase of fresh flowers. As a customer service rep you're going want to make a great first impression. You look them in the eye as you welcome them. You're efficient and helpful with the standard formalities: you've already filled out all the customer's personal details that you know from their reservation. Your aim is to simplify and speed up the process (see also Rule 3). You greet your customers just as warmly as you would your best friend.

Make sure you greet your customers with some genuine emotion rather than going through the motions. The key is to put them, rather than the act of registration, front and center. When a guest finally arrived at the five-star hotel where they'd booked a room, after a grueling trip that took more than three hours because of traffic jams, the doorman had his back turned, kept talking to a co-worker and never acknowledged their arrival.

Then, the receptionist only did the bare minimum: asked for the guest's name, handed over a key and a form to fill out, and gave directions on how to get to the room. She was friendly, but not particularly helpful. The customer experience was just as personal as it would have been if the guest had checked in online. Yet, the receptionist could have made all the difference by emotionally connecting with this guest. Instead of prioritizing function (checking in), she should have approached the guest as a human being above all else.

It doesn't matter whether it's your first encounter or a repeat. You should always try to create a warm, emotional click with the customer that stays with them. Turn a business transaction into a personal meeting. To this end, Zappos' call center representatives are trained to spot signals that can help them turn a business call into a personal call. If a rep hears a dog barking in the background or a child crying, they will respond to this to create a personal connection. Obviously, any functional aspect needs to be in order. Every action needs to be correct and efficient, so your customers are served well and right away. However, providing such service will only earn you a 6 or 7 rating. To turn a customer into a fan, you need to bring your A-game. Show an interest in them, ask how they're doing, how their kids are, make some small talk and use the information you have. People always appreciate it if you recognize them. We've seen many a pro service rep put this into practice, and to great effect. It works!

Note that authenticity is important in this. Your customers need to feel that your welcome is genuine, that your friendliness and attention are real, not fake. Reading from a script kills the customer experience, because a fixed script depersonalizes the experience. "Good morning, XYZ Hotel, my name is John Meyer, how can I help you?" This greeting seems okay, until your customers hear it for the third time and start to get irritated. So find your own way to personalize your service. If you watch the Humorous WestJet Flight Attendant video on YouTube, you'll see what we mean. His approach may not be totally suitable for your job, but you'll notice it's original and innovative.

Another important pointer is to take time for your customers. Several surveys on customer preferences regarding waiting times show that customers prefer 'being helped well' and 'allowing enough time and attention during the conversation' to 'being helped quickly'. Many indicated that they'd rather wait longer to be helped well, than be helped right away but in a rushed manner. The moral of the story: take your time when serving a customer! Whether it's on the phone, at your desk, or when making a house call, always give your customers the time they need. Sometimes, this can be hard when there's another ten people in line. But remember that customers prefer attention to shorter waiting times.

Welcome notes can be an important part of making your guests feel appreciated. Almost every high-class hotel uses welcome notes in their guest rooms. Most use printed cards or impersonal standard notes that do not mention their guests by name. They're nice, but not very distinctive anymore and a little too easy. The trick is to turn the note into something special. Figure 12 shows a note found in a room in Milan's Melia Hotel.

You can imagine that a handwritten note like this helps to give your guest a real sense of welcome.

Finally, a word about your customers' departure. A welcoming attitude is not just important when you first meet the customer, but also when they leave. A growing number of organizations

MELIÃ

MILANO
ITALY

meliahotels.com

Milan, 14 February 2018

Welcome to meliã Milano Mr Opstal!
To those who seek, even though they do not find.
To those who advance even if they get lost.
To those who share their happiness.
To those who love with madness.
Happy Valentine's day!

Jessica
guest experience

FIGURE 12. A Personalized Note

give out goodie bags (with an apple or a bottle of water) to their customers when they depart. And think of how different the customer must feel if you push their purchases over the counter, or if you get up, walk around the counter and hand them a bag carefully filled with their items. Make it World-Class Service by holding the carrying straps out, so the customer can easily take the bag from you, and top it off by holding the door open for them.

5.5. NON-VERBAL COMMUNICATION

Another important aspect of welcoming the customer is non-verbal communication, or body language. The 7-38-55-

model[19] may apply here. This model teaches us that only 7% of what we want to convey is communicated in words, 38% in our tone, and a whopping 55% in body language. Even if you say you're not angry, your eyes, eyebrows and tense muscles can betray your real emotions. Likewise, you might pretend to be interested, but your body language will reveal that you're actually in a rush to get away. So it's important to match your gestures to your words and message. The effectiveness of your message depends on consistency. Your verbal (45%) and non-verbal (55%) communication need to be in agreement. A natural smile, a pleasant handshake (firm, but not painful), eye contact, a friendly wave: these are all positive body language expressions that can reinforce your message when used appropriately.

Figure 13 shows eight simple, non-verbal signals that can reinforce the customer's experience of a warm reception. These are not only relevant to a first encounter. They can have a positive impact on any contact with your customers or co-workers.

Let's look at gestures in a little more detail. Ever had an Italian customer? They're known for their tendency to communicate with their hands. Often, their hand gestures speak louder than their voice. Be careful, however, because gestures can mean quite different things in different cultures! For example, scratching your chin might be a completely innocent act to you, but it can express something like "go to hell" in Italy. That's probably not something you'd ever want to say to a customer. But you can use gestures to your advantage. The right gesture at the right moment is a very powerful aid. But again, watch out. Some hand motions signal narrow-mindedness, while others indicate openness and a welcoming attitude. For instance, pointing with your index finger is a domineering or accusing gesture. An open hand, with your palm turned upwards, is much friendlier.

1. **55% of what you communicate is non-verbal**
2. **Non-verbal communications have a great impact on the warmth you project**
3. **Keep in mind possible cultural differences**

In *Be Our Guest* (see 'Read More' at the end of this chapter), Theodore Kinni describes how Disney employees give park visitors directions to get to a particular ride or location. They use an open hand, palm up, fingers stretched to show them the way. That's a much friendlier gesture than a closed fist from which an index finger jerkily, almost militarily, points in the right direction. Disney is very aware of this kind of detail in communicating with guests verbally and non-verbally. Its customer service policies are also inspired by the diversity of its visitors: the organization takes great effort to treat all its visitors respectfully.

And lastly, your distance to the customer and the spot where you stand have an effect on how your customer feels. Many hotels have a reception desk, which positions the receptionist opposite the customer, with quite a gap (and a desk) between the two. There is another way. Some hotels have done away with the desk. They ask their new arrivals to take a seat on a couch in the lounge.

The receptionist then sits next to them, offers them a drink and helps them to check in using a tablet computer. The same trend is happening in offices; reception desks are being removed and receptionists are becoming hosts who receive visitors standing up and offer them a cup of coffee while they wait for their appointment. What a difference that makes.

	Aspects	Tips
1	Smiles & eye contact	- If you don't make eye contact, you may appear insecure - Preferably smile after making eye contact; this appears more personal - Use eye contact in moderation (Eastern cultures may find eye contact aggressive) As usual, a little goes a long way. - Excessively long-lasting or intense eye contact can send a totally different message than friendliness
2	Vibe	- Pretend you're meeting a friend: you'll appear more relaxed - Act calmly, not nervously - Staring can look like absentmindedness - If you constantly look at your notes, you may appear ill-prepared or uninterested
3	Personal space	- Use your personal space - If you slouch, you make a bad impression. Stand straight with your shoulders back.
4	Head position	- Don't stare down, hold your head up high, chin up, and look your customer in the eye
5	Posture	- Stand on both legs, don't stand on one leg or lean to one side - Lean slightly forward if that helps you - Don't lean against anything (this makes you look lazy)
6	Movement	- Move toward your customer when you're talking to them - Control your movements - Quick little movements convey nervousness. Controlled movements express control over the situation.
7	Hands	- Don't fold your hands, pick your nails, wiggle your fingers or adjust your watch, rings or eyeglasses - Keep your hands next to your body in a relaxed pose - Putting one hand in a pocket is sometimes okay, but never put both hands in your pockets (total no-no) - Don't cross your arms (this expresses distance)
8	Gestures	- Hand gestures are important - Be aware of international differences in the meaning of gestures

FIGURE 13. Aspects of Non-Verbal Communication.

5.6. IN SHORT

First impressions count. They have great impact on customers, especially on demanding customers. First impressions are formed even before your actual first encounter with the customer. You can make use of this knowledge by preventing stress in the run-up to that first encounter, and by being aware that customers may be carrying negative emotional 'baggage' from earlier contact. Make sure you notice, recognize and acknowledge your customers. Customers like to be addressed by their name whenever possible. Roll out the red carpet for your customers, so to speak, and give them genuine attention. Take your time and remember that a large part of your communication with them consists of non-verbal clues.

REALITY CHECK

- What does your red carpet look like? What first impression do you make? What are your strengths and what can you improve?
- Do you notice your customers right away? Do you know their name before they introduce themselves?
- Do you get enough time to give your customers the attention they deserve? How can you free up more time?
- How is your non-verbal communication? Does it make your customers feel welcome?
- Are you sensitive to cultural differences in communication?

READ MORE

Contact: The First Four Minutes
Leonard Zunin and Natalie Zunin – ISBN 9780840212887

First Impressions: What You Don't Know about How Others See You
Ann Demarais, Valerie White – ISBN 9780553803204

Lessons from the Mouse
Dennis Snow – ISBN 9780615372419

Be Our Guest; Perfecting the Art of Customer Service
Disney Institute & Theodore Kinni – ISBN 978 1423145844

6 COVER THE BASICS

6.1. INTRODUCTION

The basics are actually the foundations of your relationship with the customer. The basics are the dissatisfiers that you have to watch out for (see Fig. 1, Section 2.3), because while they can't produce happy customers, they can result in dissatisfied and even highly emotional, negative customer responses. Certainly when it comes to demanding customers, failing to meet their expectations can have a big impact on their reactions. And remember: in their experience, a factor is more readily a dissatisfier. The basics, in combination with Rule 1 – Make Customers Feel Welcome – are the foundations upon which you base your entire attitude and all your conduct. If you haven't covered the basics yet, start there. If you regularly get below-par scores from your customers, negative comments or even complaints about the way you function, you need to get your basics up to scratch.

The basics are extremely important to customers. They are what help them decide whether you are their go-to service provider.

In other words, the basics largely determine whether a customer even wants to do business with you at all. Bear in mind that the customer's impressions are not necessarily a reflection of reality. You might have great expertise, but if the customer thinks you don't (or thinks you're showing off), then that is the customer's truth. So, take that difference into account. Reality and the customer's perception are not always the same.

FIGURE 14. The Four Aspects of Rule 2, Cover the Basics

Figure 14 shows which aspects of this rule you need to get right. It all begins with reliably sticking to agreements you've made. Other aspects are your expertise (competence) and efficiency. Your outward appearance, what the customer sees when they look at you, is a factor, too. And the last aspect is how you conduct yourself in terms of integrity and ethics. In short, these four basics are the foundations of the customer experience.

6.2. RELIABILITY

Customers want to know what they can expect. They want to know what you and your colleagues are going to do. They want

to make concrete agreements that they can count on. Reliability starts with reaching specific, measurable, achievable, realistic and time-bound (SMART) agreements. Demanding customers do not accept 'I'll do my best' or, worse, 'I can't make any promises'. They want concrete promises, sometimes even in black and white. That can be pretty hard to give them, especially when customers demand them here and now. And actually, you shouldn't make promises unless you are 100% sure you can deliver.
You might find yourself in a situation where you have to make a promise which you can only make good on, if some third party also keeps their promises to you. Therefore, always check with this co-worker first to be sure they will deliver to you, before making any hard promises to the customer. It's better not to make any concrete promises than to fail to deliver on one.

1. **Make clear agreements**
2. **Only make promises you can keep**
3. **An agreement is an agreement**
4. **If you won't be able to deliver, contact the customer**
5. **Help the customer even when someone else has failed to do their job**

Customers want you to stick to what you have agreed on. 'A deal's a deal' is probably the most important basic of them all. 'Say what you do and do what you say' is another well-known phrase. If you don't honor your agreements, you will quickly lose the confidence of your customer. They will no longer feel like you take them seriously, and this will likely lead to a complaint. So, if you know you regrettably won't be able to keep your end of the deal, be the one to get in touch. Contact the customer as soon as you can, and say it like it is. Tell them what they can expect from you. Avoid the 'squeaky wheel syndrome' where you only respond to customers who complain (squeak), because then you're too late.

So what do you do when one of your co-workers or even another department of your company failed to meet their side of an agreement? If you are the person who is in direct contact with the customer, keep in mind that you are the organization's calling card. The customer expects you to pick up the ball that others dropped, to solve the problem. Tell yourself: the buck stops here. A demanding customer is not helped when you forward the call to someone else or refer them to another department. You are, at that moment, their point of contact. Take responsibility, don't wait for someone else to do it. Just do it yourself. And do it immediately, because speedy action and speedy results are part of the customer experience.

Once upon a time, there were three people: SOMEONE, EVERYONE and NO ONE. One day, there was an important job to do. EVERYONE was asked to do it. But EVERYONE thought that SOMEONE else would do it. And even though EVERYONE could do it, NO ONE did.

This made SOMEONE angry, because it was EVERYONE'S job and NO ONE had done it. EVERYONE thought that SOMEONE should have done it, but NO ONE had realized that EVERYONE was unwilling to do it.

In the end, EVERYONE blamed SOMEONE, because NO ONE did what EVERYONE could have done.

Remember: 'underpromise, overdeliver'. Doing what you promised to do, but doing it better or faster, is always good.

6.3. EXPERTISE & EFFICIENCY

We know from customer surveys that customers – when pushed to make a choice – prefer a service rep with expertise over a friendly services rep. Their reason is usually something like this: 'What good is a friendly employee if they can't help me?' The main thing customers want is service. Fast, efficient check-in, an accurate answer to their question, a real solution to their problem, being served a meal correctly, a wine recommendation that really pairs with the food. In short, an employee without knowledge and experience does not have the basics down. That's why Singapore Airlines only lets its new cabin personnel work in-flight after several months of training. Customers should never be subjected to the mistakes of someone who's still in training.

Expertise consists of knowledge and skills that are acquired through experience and personal development. Therefore, it's important to become knowledgeable and skilled before you go 'on stage.' Know how to do your job, feel comfortable with the required tasks, and understand what you need to do in the situations you will encounter. Learning should happen off stage, before you come into contact with customers. Of course, there are situations which you can only learn in practice, but understanding how the computer software in your hotel works is not something you should be learning while trying to help a guest check in. That's off-stage stuff.

The expertise we're talking about can be divided into three areas: the job, the product and the organization. The first of these is the expertise in your daily work that leads to efficiency. You need to know the methods required, understand the IT and communication tech, be aware of the rules and the social mores, and be so well-versed in all of these that you can do your job well, and efficiently, in one go. Demanding customers are often in a rush. They probably won't mind waiting just a bit, but not if they see you fumble while they wait. Your service should be fast, efficient, and on the money. That's what it's all about. So, practice whatever it is you do to the point where you know you'll get it right when you're 'on stage', serving real customers.

The second area of expertise is the product or service provided by your organization. You need to be able to describe it, and to answer questions the customer asks about it. If you work in a restaurant, you have to know the ingredients in all the dishes and which allergies might be relevant. If you work at hotel reception, you have to know the answers to the thirty or forty most frequently asked questions about the hotel's services and products. FAQs should also be discussed by the whole team.
The third area of expertise involves knowledge of the organization. You should know who does what in your organization, and what people's responsibilities are. This means that when you are unable to help a customer, you know who to turn to. And if you don't know, don't just fumble about. Admit to the customer that you don't know yet who can help, but that you will find the answer and get back to them promptly. Every customer understands that no one knows everything and will forgive you for having to consult others for an answer to their unusual question. Just make sure you get back to the customer quickly.

1. **Know your job, product and organization**
2. **Handle matters efficiently and effectively**
3. **Provide correct information**
4. **Know your limitations**
5. **Learn off stage instead of burdening the customer**

6.4. OUTWARD APPEARANCE

All people, customers included, form an opinion of the person standing before them within the first seconds of their first meeting (see Rule 1). If you are a doctor, but you walk around in a t-shirt and jeans, then this makes a very different impression than if you wear a white lab coat. If you're standing behind the reception desk in a uniform covered in stains, your customers will draw different conclusions about you then if you are dressed in a spotless, pressed attire. A tiny mistake, a detail, can make a customer hesitant or even worried. Your clothing and appearance have more influence on customers than you think. It does depend what kind of organization you work for, of course. If you work for a trendy ad agency or restaurant, the customer will expect something else from you than from someone working at a traditional accountancy firm or dining establishment. But wherever you work, your attire must be spotlessly clean. Whether it should be classic, modern, trendy, cheery, casual, understated – that's something your organization has probably given some thought to.

1. **Spotless clothing that matches your organization's image**
2. **Well-fitted attire**
3. **Personal care**

Be sure that your clothing is in tiptop shape. No buttons missing, no stains, shoes polished, everything neatly tucked in. If you wear a company uniform, wear the right size. Nothing is more annoying than wearing clothes that are too tight, or too loose. It will bother you, and you can't help but show this irritation, so your customer will notice that right away.

Customers will also have thoughts about your personal care. The basics are simple: good hygiene and a fresh smell. If you perspire a lot while working, have a change of clothing with you to put on halfway through the shift. Organizations all have their own rules about your personal appearance. They have different norms concerning hairstyles, beards, earrings and other visible piercings and tattoos. Customers have different opinions about these things, too. But you can be sure that many companies with demanding customers have strict rules in this regard. They want to avoid any kind of negative customer experience.

☐ 6.5. INTEGRITY AND ETHICS

The last of the four basics is your own conduct towards the customer. Don't do unto others what you don't want others to do unto you. This code for integrity and ethical conduct has a number of consequences.

One of the first considerations has to do with how you handle private data about your customers. Years ago, we talked to a client of an accountancy firm who told us he had decided to move his business to a firm on the other side of the country. He took this step because his previous accountant in his own hometown had freely shared private information about him and his business with others. That's how important privacy is. It's a shame that a customer has to take their business somewhere far away because a professional failed to act with integrity. To put it briefly, use discretion when dealing with your customers' information. Don't share it with other customers, friends, or acquaintances. Don't even share it with co-workers if it is not relevant to them. If you do, you are putting yourself at risk of losing your customers' trust. Discretion also means you must take great care when entering private data in systems that others have access to. A customer that has shared confidential information with you might be unpleasantly surprised to hear your colleague mention that information on a day when you aren't working. Data management rules are closely tied to legislation, and breaking these rules can lead to harsh punishment (see Sections 8.4 and 8.5).

1. **Show integrity when dealing with customers' data**
2. **Show your customers respect, don't discriminate**
3. **Don't treat your customers in a way that you would not want to be treated yourself**

Another aspect of integrity and ethical conduct is fighting discrimination. Treat customers with respect, regardless of their sex, race, orientation, religion or age. None of these factors should affect your actions or decisions negatively. Of course, you can take these things into account to deliver even better service. One example is asking an elderly customer who might have trouble with something whether you can do anything extra to help them.

Finally, integrity and ethical conduct is about not doing anything that you can't answer for to yourself. You do business and make decisions that are in the organization's and the customer's interests. You don't sell the customer anything that is not good for them. The customer's interests come before your own in this respect. And you should not make decisions based solely on what's legal or on the organization's goals. Making ethical choices means taking everyone's rights, interests, desires and societal considerations into account. Honesty is the best policy, after all.

6.6. IN SHORT

Excellent service starts with getting the basics down, all the things a customer expects. And not all customers are the same; a demanding customer expects more than an easygoing one. The basics are the dissatisfiers, actually. Doing your job right does not necessarily earn you any points, but not doing it right does tend to lead to dissatisfaction and criticism. One of the basics is reliability: saying what you do, and doing what you say.

And if you're unable to keep a promise, take immediate action. Customers don't like to see incompetence, so be sure you have the necessary knowledge and skills about your job, the product and the organization. Your appearance, your personal hygiene and the way you dress, may influence how the customer sees you. So, take care of your appearance and wear spotless clothing.
Lastly, the customer expects you to conduct yourself with integrity and never to discriminate. Again, you should see this list of basics as an initial 'license to operate'. If you tick these boxes, you won't get any compliments or applause, but you also won't be flooded with complaints from dissatisfied customers.

REALITY CHECK

- Do you make clear agreements with customers?
- Do you live by the phrase 'a deal is a deal'?
- Do you have the knowledge and skills to help the customer efficiently and effectively?
- Is your personal care and attire top-notch?
- Do you always show integrity when dealing with a customer's private information?

READ MORE

Be on Your Best Business Behavior: How to Avoid Social and Professional Faux Pas
Colleen Rickenbacher – ISBN 9780978764210

Ethics and Customer Service
Thomas C. Reischl – ISBN 9780872186736

7

MAKE LIFE EASIER FOR THE CUSTOMER

7.1. INTRODUCTION

If you tell a supermarket shopper to "Check in aisle 4 or 5. End of this aisle and then take a right", or ask a newly-arrived hotel guest to fill in an endless form, you're quite likely to offend these customers. Demanding customers don't like unnecessary work. They neither understand nor accept that you can't be bothered to show them where the product is, or copy their personal details from the reservation. After all, that's your job, right? And there is another way. If you escort the customer to the right aisle, you make their life a lot easier. Just like pre-filling the form for your hotel guest takes work off their hands. Excellent service means shouldering the burden for the customer, making things easier by making sure the customer doesn't have to deal with any unnecessary hassles. It's not only a matter of simplifying things, but also of relieving the customer of possible worries or stress.

We've divided this third rule, making life easier for the customer, into four aspects: providing certainty, eliminating hassle, simplifying actions, and preventing the next problem by means of 'forward resolution' (see Fig. 15).

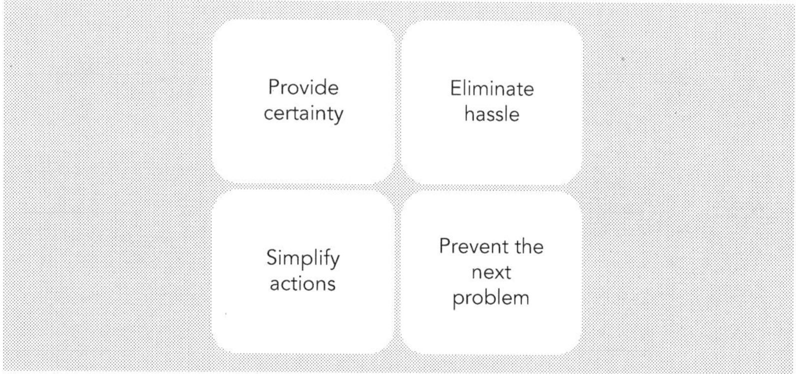

FIGURE 15. The Four Aspects of Rule 3, Make Life Easier for the Customer

7.2. PROVIDE CERTAINTY BY BEING PROACTIVE

An accountancy firm client has received a warning from the Tax Authority for being late filing their VAT return and paying the amount due. If they're late again next time, the client will be given a stiff fine. So when it's time to file the next VAT return, the client emails all the necessary information to the accountant, well in advance of the deadline. But they receive no reply, not even an automatic response: no sign whatsoever that the accountant has seen the information and is on it. This leaves the client in uncertainty. Finally, after a long wait, the client calls the accountant and is told that all the paperwork will be processed on time. The client gets the accountant to agree to send a standard acknowledgement of receipt and a timeline showing when the job will be completed.

Customers often rank clear communication in the top 3 of qualities they consider important in customer service. However, wherever people work, cooperate, and deal with customers, there are uncertainties. When are they coming? What time? How long will I have to wait in line? Has the receptionist even noticed me? Did they receive my payment? Is the flight canceled or not, and if so, what do I do? These questions lead to uncertainty and even stress. True, there are all kinds of automated systems like tracking & tracing that inform customers on the status of their order, complaint, etc. That helps. But as a customer service rep you can help even more. Think about what uncertainties your customers are dealing with and what you could do to relieve their stress. For one, you could get in touch with the customer to give them information before they start getting too uneasy. You could let that customer who's been waiting in line know that you're aware they're there. Little moves like these can go a long way towards relieving the uncertainty a customer feels.

1. **Know when your customers feel uncertain**
2. **Proactively intervene to relieve this feeling**

7.3. ELIMINATE HASSLE

Customers who are in a rush don't understand why they have to jump through hoops. Why do they have to fill in another form? Your organization has this information already! Why do they have to go to another representative? Why not help them yourself, so they don't have to go stand in another line and explain the whole thing again. Why do they need to make another call, why are they the one that has to call back? Many organizations require their customers to do things that are totally unnecessary. Why do they make such demands when they are perfectly capable of handling these tasks themselves?

Demanding customers are particularly allergic to this. And you can prevent the problem altogether—and leave your customers satisfied—by taking the hassle off their hands.

This starts with simply not asking the customer for information that you already have. Or if you give them a form, at least fill in all the information which you already know for sure. Don't force the customer to show all kinds of proof. This alone will pre-empt a lot of 'complaining' from demanding customers.

A guest at a luxury hotel calls reception to request an extra-large towel. How would you reply? "Of course, you can come pick it up at reception," or do you ask the duty manager to bring one up to the room? And when will the towel get there? A half-hour after the phone call? Five minutes after the call? When does the customer need the towel?
Make things as pleasant and simple as possible for the customer. Convenience is quickly becoming a dissatisfier for demanding customers. Make it as easy as possible for them. The less effort it takes the customer to get what they want, the better. So, maybe it's an idea to make the extra-large towel standard in all the rooms?

Linate Airport Hotel in Milan is a great example of a hotel that works according to this rule. The hotel itself is nothing special. It's very basic, and past its prime. But what is uncommon about it is the receptionist. If you arrive there for a second visit (because it's so conveniently situated near the airport which is great for a morning flight), you're greeted with a warm smile: "Welcome back,

Mr Opstal, it's so nice to have you with us again. This is your key. Do you need help with your luggage?
Well, enjoy your stay." When you book a hotel room there, you don't need to fill in any forms or give your credit card number for possible additional charges. It's fast. Walk in, get your key, go to your room. Simple. And... everything in the minibar is free. No 6 euros for a bottle of water. Again, it's not an unusual hotel. It just offers really good service. It doesn't have five stars, but its employees are just that: stars. Every one of them. People make all the difference!

Customers love convenience, both in terms of action and thought. People tend to take the path of least resistance and do things on automatic pilot. So, if you want to get the customer to do something, you should appeal to their automatic pilot mode. When customers are forced to fill out a form, many will refuse. No matter how interesting the form is. Why? Because filling out a form takes time and energy. We've learned a lot about this in recent years from the field of behavioral economics[20]. A lot of our behavior is not determined by our rational mind and conscious action (System 2 thinking), but by our emotions and intuition (System 1 thinking). Much customer behavior, therefore, is intuitive rather than conscious. System 1 is our favorite mode because it takes less energy. We love convenience and ease, we detest unnecessary hassles.

System 1 Thinking

- Fast
- Characteristics: unconscious, automatic, effortless
- Without awareness or control: 'What you see, is what you get.'
- Role: evaluating the situation and giving updates
- Comprises 98% of our thinking

System 2 Thinking

- Slow
- Characteristics: well-considered and conscious, controlled, a thought process that requires effort and rationality
- Uses awareness and control: logic and skepticism
- Role: searches for new/missing information, makes decisions
- Comprises 2% of our thinking

1. **Customers love convenience**
2. **Don't expect them to do what they consider a hassle**
3. **Self-service is good, but don't overdo it**

Why, if we know that customers want convenience and hate hassle, do so many organizations make things difficult for the customer and saddle them with so many unnecessary tasks? There are two reasons for this: distrust of the customer and the desire for increased efficiency.

Some organizations fundamentally distrust their customers. Because 1 out of 100 customers somehow abuses the system, the other 99 have to pay for it. But there is another way. Trust the customer, show good faith until they prove themself unworthy of it. A great example of this is that some insurance companies no longer require policyholders to show unreasonable amounts of evidence before they compensate damage. They trust their customers. You, too, can do the same thing. Avoid making your customers carry out unnecessary tasks.

In certain sectors, self-service has become synonymous with convenience. But sometimes it seems like the entire planet is embracing self-service. More and more, businesses are shifting the burden to the customer. We're not talking about companies like IKEA, whose customers appreciate the fact that they can do a lot themselves because they know it keeps the price down. What we're saying is that self-service should not become the norm in all situations. We see customers frequently being saddled with tasks because the company distrusts them or wants to cut costs. But all too often, they're subjecting their customers to something they don't want.

The second reason companies often shift the administrative burden to customers is the idea that this is more efficient and cuts costs. "Just fill out this form, that makes it easier for us to help you." Yeah, right. Managers and IT people are kidding themselves if they think customers don't mind this. Nothing could be further from the truth. Of course, customers do understand service is not the same everywhere and that more is required of them in budget supermarkets, budget hotels and other businesses that offer low-priced services and goods. After all, customers know they save money from the formula in which only the bare basic product is provided (this, too, is a choice). But don't try this in mid-range or high-end segments. Here, too, customer service reps can make a difference. Don't make your customer call you back, call them. Hold the door open for your customer. In general, take a few days to analyze what it is you do on a daily basis. In which situations do you have the customer do things that you yourself would not appreciate having to do? Look for the red tape that you would not want to have to deal with. The norm should be: 'Is it logical that the customer has to do this?' And 'is it absolutely necessary that the customer does it?'

7.4. SIMPLIFY ACTIONS

Aside from taking work off your customer's hands, there are other things you can do to make life easier for them. Here are some examples of successful simplifications. One click orders. If you create an account in an online store, all your personal and payment details are stored, so for your next order all you have to do is log in and click the button to order a product. And if you order before 11 p.m., your product will be delivered to your door the very next morning. License plate recognition has made driving out of a parking garage much easier. No more stopping the car, removing the seatbelt and leaning out of the window to reach the card reader. When frequent fliers check in with their favorite airline, the card number is all it takes for ground crew to see whether they prefer a window seat.

These are all examples of how organizations can use technology to make things easier for the customer. As a customer service rep, you, too, can play a role in this, as the following example illustrates. One day, at Roomers Hotel in Baden Baden, the hotel manager waited out front to personally welcome a guest. After taking a shower, the guest was headed for a dinner date near the casino, when he overheard two other guests asking the receptionist to order a taxi. He quickly asked for a second taxi for himself: "You're calling anyway, so perhaps you could just order two taxis instead of one." The hotel manager overheard this and stepped in, insisting on driving all three guests to their destinations.

1. **Sometimes it's unavoidable that something is required of a customer**
2. **When that happens, make it easier for them**

7.5. FORWARD RESOLUTION: PREVENT THE NEXT PROBLEM

Finally, we will point out how your proactiveness can ensure your customers won't have to deal with physical or mental tasks in the future. Answer the question before it is asked. Be one step ahead of the customer by thinking ahead. Anticipate. What questions, problems or worries might the customer have next? By thinking this through ahead of time, you'll be able to say to the customer: "I've already taken care of that for you." Put yourself in your customers' shoes and think about what they will be doing or dealing with next. Have they already mentioned any problems, and have these been dealt with? What might be their next problem? Mention it, help them resolve it at an early stage, or better yet before it actually occurs. And let them know you've done so, if this information is relevant to them (forward resolution).

1. **Identify possible questions, problems and worries the customer might have next**
2. **Mention them to your customer**
3. **Try to prevent or resolve them**

7.6. IN SHORT

People like being on automatic pilot (System 1 Thinking), because this takes the least energy. They like convenience because it makes things simpler and relieves them of hassles. Demanding customers have great expectations in this area. Step up so customers don't have to experience any unnecessary worries about your service, avoid asking them to do anything that isn't strictly necessary,

and, when something is unavoidable, make it as easy as possible. In some cases, you know from experience that customers might run into some kind of problem next. So alert them, or better yet, ensure that the problem doesn't occur.
This will spare you a lot of headaches later on.

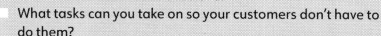

REALITY CHECK

- In what situations can you take away your customers' uncertainties?
- Do you trust your customers, or distrust them? What effect does this have?
- What tasks can you take on so your customers don't have to do them?
- How can you make things easier for your customers?
- How can you apply 'forward resolution' for your customers?

READ MORE

Thinking, Fast and Slow
Daniel Kahneman – ISBN 9780374533557

Predictably Irrational: The Hidden Forces That Shape Our Decisions
Dan Ariely – ISBN 9780007256532

The Effortless Experience
Matthew Dixon – ISBN 9780241003305

8 CUSTOMIZE YOUR SERVICE

8.1. INTRODUCTION

A guest at a Ritz Carlton hotel in the US goes for a jog every morning. When he returns, he likes to drink water and eat a banana. Not an apple. A year later, he stays at a Ritz Carlton in Germany. To his delight, the receptionist asks him during check-in whether he plans to go jogging in the morning and whether he'd like extra water in his room? "Yes... please! Thank you," he stammers. He goes to his room and finds water and bananas there. Not apples. Later, he asks a hotel employee. "How did you know?"
Ritz Carlton is great when it comes to service. When rooms are being cleaned in the morning, a housekeeping employee comes in and just observes. Which radio station does this guest listen to? What fruit do they eat? Does this guest use extra towels? Are there sports garments hanging out to dry? Housekeeping notes down these details and tells reception. The information helps the hotel make guests feel as comfortable as possible.

By being so attentive, the Ritz Carlton makes customer contact more personal. In every single hotel in that chain, you notice how they're living their slogan: 'We're ladies and gentlemen serving ladies and gentlemen.'

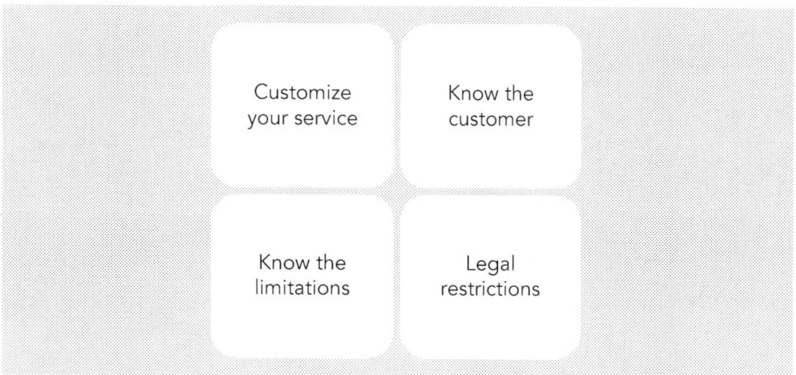

FIGURE 16. The Four Aspects of Rule 4, Customize your Service

This fourth rule is about personalizing the service you provide by knowing your customers and tailoring your service to them. Doing this gives customers the feeling that they are known, important, and particularly, not just a number or anonymous person. In this chapter, we describe customization of service based on knowing your customers. But we also look at the limitations of this approach. Customers sometimes experience customization as pushy, and tailoring service can even have negative consequences for the customer. In addition, there are legal restrictions that have to be taken into account.

8.2. CUSTOMIZING YOUR SERVICE

Imagine that you visit a big law firm for the second time and have to wait at reception. The receptionist asks, "I hope you didn't get stuck in that traffic jam. I see that you have an appointment with Ms Thomas. I've already told her you're here." And then, "Would you like a cup of coffee? No milk, two sugars, right?" When you leave, the receptionist hands you a goody bag: a bottle of water, an apple and a chocolate chip cookie. The firm knows you love that. The bag also contains two little toys for your kids, because the firm also remembers that you have two children who love Lego.

You might think you don't have enough information about your customers to offer them tailored service. But you have more than you realize. Your business knows a lot about return customers (see Section 8.3). If that customer has been welcomed and registered properly, you already know them. By knowing the customer, you can be much more proactive in your contact with them and offer them the custom service experience. Does the customer have a family? Children? What are their hobbies? How does the customer drink their coffee or tea? Earl Grey? Milk and sugar? Cookie? If you're dealing with a very important customer, why not make use of your knowledge about these preferences? As long as you do it subtly and it enhances the customer's experience in a positive way. Leave fresh flowers in the room, for instance. Do they have meal preferences, or allergies you know about? When was the last time the customer and your organization were in contact? What was discussed? By building on this knowledge and using it appropriately, you can give the customer a warm, welcoming sensation. The better hotels check every day which guests will be coming in the days ahead. Then, they look up the personal preferences of each of these guests in their computer system, and/or on social media. They try to integrate this knowledge actively, but discretely, into their service. Examples include: reserving the guest's favorite room, remembering what they drink and which magazines they read and leaving these items in the room, etc. This information also comes in handy when writing a personal welcome note in the room (A warm welcome to you, Congratulations, Happy Holidays, etc.).

1. **Customers like customized service, because it makes them feel important, known, recognized**
2. **Use what you know about the customer to customize your service**

To train employees in selling a new product, a motorcycle manufacturer rents out a beautiful hotel in Spain, where dealers and sales managers will watch three days of presentations on the latest model. Aside from this classical training, there will also be dynamic sessions in which the attendees can also experience the new motorbike on public roads and a racetrack.
When they arrive, they are greeted by invitingly shiny motorbikes in all imaginable colors, neatly parked and waiting to be driven. What's more, the event is superbly catered. In short, the company spared no expense. But what makes this training event so special is the phenomenal attention to detail. The credit card-type room keys sport the brand logo on one side and an image of the new model on the other. Each guest finds in their own room a selection of magazines that appeal to their personal interests (such as cars and motorcycles). All the menus in the hotel restaurant carry the brand logo, too. It's even projected onto the façade of the hotel every evening, and all hotel employees wear a logo lapel pin. They've thought of everything. But the best thing of all is the wi-fi, which uses the model number of the new motorbike as the password to get online.

8.3. KNOW YOUR CUSTOMERS

Custom service is only possible when you know your customer. Organizations that excel at this, use a structured CSUM-cycle (Collect-Store-Use-Maintain). We described Use in the previous section, so now we will discuss the other three components.

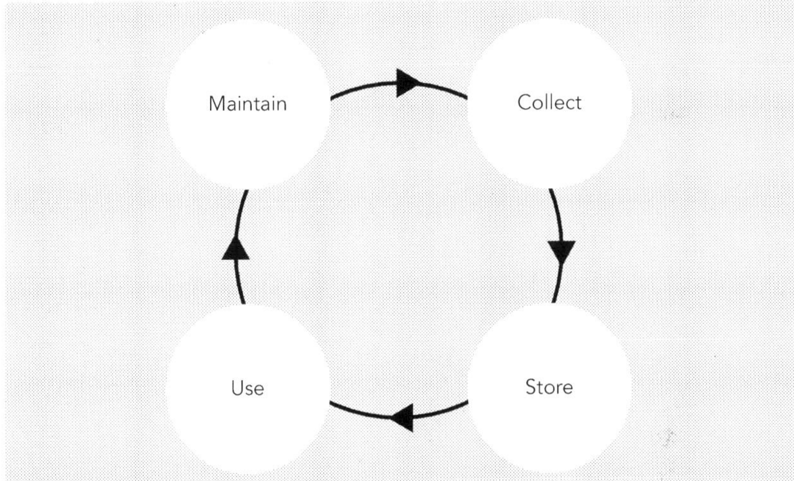

FIGURE 17. CSUM Cycle

Collect

If you want to offer personalized, tailored service, you must begin with the way you collect information about your customers which you will later put to use. Of course, many companies buy all kinds of customer data, but the type of information you need in order to personalize service is often not included in that purchased data. You play an important role in picking up signals and looking for relevant information. There are four categories of information: contact history, explicit signals, implicit signals and information you yourself have detected.

Contact history is an important category. Whenever you speak to the customer, receive an email from them, field a complaint, talk to them on the phone, or have any other kind of interaction, note this down. This gives you and your co-workers a chance to bring it up the next time you speak to the same customer. A demanding customer expects you to be aware of what has happened in previous encounters with your company.

Sometimes you receive customer information on a silver platter, so to speak, when customers tell you specifically what they expect (explicit signals). The rock band Van Halen, for instance, had a contractual list of demands for all the hotels where they stayed. There had to be M&Ms available at all times, but only specific colors of M&Ms. The main reason for this bizarre M&M clause was to enable lawyers to check whether the other party had read the contract carefully and paid attention to detail. Beyoncé, for her part, used to insist on an exact room temperature and absolutely no Coca Cola products (at the time, she had a deal with Pepsi). Adele is said to have a long list of demands, including six metal spoons and six large tea mugs. Mariah Carey insists on having specific beverages in her room as well as sugar-free chewing gum, and rumor has it that Will Ferrell explicitly asked to be supplied with an electric tricycle. It gets even more bizarre. Pharrell Williams reportedly demands that a portrait of his favorite astronomer be hung in his hotel room (see text box on p. 108-9[21]).

1. **Actively listen/look for implicit signals**
2. **Note these down, along with contact history, explicit signals and any other information you have picked up on**
3. **Keep this information up to date; outdated information is highly risky**

Pharrell Williams' personal demands

DRESSING ROOM #I (Pharrell Williams)

- 1 Trash Can lined with Trash Bag
- Plates, Bowls, Napkins, Forks, Knives, Spoons, Wine glasses, Hot Cups, and 1 package of plastic 16 oz Cups (500ml) to cater for 20 people
- Disposable Knives/Forks/Spoons
- 1 Bottle Opener
- 1 Corkscrew
- 1 Tabasco/Hot Sauce
- 1 box of matches (Very Important)
- 1 Sharp Metal Knife and Clean Cutting Board
- 1 Case (24 bottles) of Alkaline Water (8 Room Temp)
- 1 Case (24 bottles) of Still Water (NO Evian/Nestle/Dasani/Aquafina) (8 Room Temp)
- 4 Cans of Red Bull (NO Sugar Free)
- 1 Large Bottle of POM Pomegranate Juice
- 1 Liter bottle of Silver Patron Tequila
- 1 Liter bottle of Kettle One Vodka
- 12 Bottles of Stella (chilled)
- 12 Cans of SUPER COLD Assorted Sodas (including Coke, Sprite & Ginger Ale)
- 6 Cans Lemon San Pellegrino
- 1 loaf of Gluten free bread
- 1 Bag of Gluten free crackers
- 1 Crunchy White Almond Butter
- 1 Bag of Raw Almonds unsalted
- 1 Grape Jelly
- Dirty Brand Potato Chips
- 1 Bag Salted Kettle Chips
- Sensible portions brand veggie straws (Ranch Flavor)
- 1 Box Nilla Wafers
- 1 Bag Goldfish
- 1 Bunch Bananas

- 5 fresh lemons
- Fresh Ginger Root
- Kettle, Mugs, Teaspoons, English Breakfast Tea, Throat Coat Tea & Fresh Cream
- 1 Regular Squeezey Honey
- 1 Manuka Honey 30+
- 1 Full-Length Mirror
- 1 Tooth Brush & Toothpaste
- 1 Framed Picture of Carl Sagan
- Pedialyte
- Cetaphil Soap Bar & Soap Dish
- Cetaphil Cleansing Wipes
- Cetaphil Cleansing Lotion
- 1 Box Tissues

Implicit signals are harder to pick up. However, if you study emails, letters and conversations, you'll notice that customers reveal a lot of information. For this, you have to have your personal antennae out, an alertness to spot new information. A customer might say they will not be present next Thursday because it's their wedding anniversary and they'll be celebrating with dinner and a show. Or perhaps the customer will mention an important meeting, or will quote an article from what they reveal to be their favorite magazine. Maybe they will mention that football is a fantastic sport. Or that they prefer their coffee black with no sugar. This is all information you can use later on.

You can also try to find this information on your own. Social media is an inexhaustible source of personal tidbits that people share with the world. You will find photos there, and all kinds of other personal details.

Store
The next thing you need to do is record and store the information you've collected so that you or a co-worker can look it up again later. It's also important that people in other departments of your organization can consult this information. Some businesses have an extensive CRM (Customer Relationship Management) system like Salesforce, ZOHO or Microsoft Dynamics 365. Others use simpler methods like an Excel tab for each customer.

In Section 8.1, we mentioned the Ritz Carlton. This chain uses a Guest History System. When a guest asks for a longer bed, they are given one of course. If the same person checks in to a Ritz Carlton on another continent the following week, the hotel will immediately offer them a long bed. How do they know this? If a guest switches beds (or rooms for that matter), the hotel notes this down in the Guest History System, which all hotels check every day. You, too, can use a system like this.

So, what information is relevant? Details like:
- Name, address and other contact details
- Contact history: list of previous contacts with the customer, description of nature of contact and result
- Complaints and outcomes of satisfaction surveys
- Hobbies and interests
- Family details, birthdays and anniversaries
- Specific preferences, dos and don'ts for this customer

Maintain
Lastly, it is important to periodically update customer information. Are the details still accurate? Is any of the information outdated? After all, it's better to have no information than outdated or incorrect information.

Mackay66

For all of his professional life, Harvey Mackay (businessman, columnist and author of *Swim with the Sharks Without Being Eaten Alive*), has used what he calls the Mackay66 within his Golden Rule: Know Your Customer. Mackay66 is an extensive questionnaire meant to gather personal data which allows him to create a customer profile. These data include:

- Name, address, place of residence
- Education
- Names of spouse and children
- Birthdays
- Previous employers
- Dietary preferences
- Cars
- Favorite vacation spot
- Religion
- Favorite drink(s)
- Etc.

P.S. Mackay66 was devised in the 1950s; today it would probably conflict with the current privacy legislation laid down in the General Data Protection Regulation (see Section 8.5.)

8.4. THERE ARE LIMITATIONS

It's often said that you should help the customer as you would like to be helped. In rule, this used to be a good basic concept. However, it is no longer applicable. It's better, nowadays, to help the customer as *they* want to be helped. Deliver personalized service, attuned to the needs and wishes of the customer in question. Your preferences are irrelevant, it's the customer's which is important. This even means that some customers don't want tailored service. They don't want to be recognized, they want anonymity. If you know this about a particular customer, provide that person with what they want. That, too, is a kind of customized service.

There are also limitations to the legal and appropriate use of customer data. The first of these is that you must always remain conscious of the types of data you should and should not record for your colleagues to see. Sensitive and confidential information is obviously not suitable for sharing or entering in a system that others can access.
The second limitation is that you must only use the information you have in an appropriate way. Always reason from the customer's perspective. After all, if they're likely to find it strange that you have a given piece of information, or if they might get a 'big brother is watching you' feeling, then using that information will backfire. In general, a regular customer is less likely to react that way than a one-off customer. In each situation, you must determine whether it is appropriate to use certain types of information. "Welcome back, Mr Smith. Would you like to start with a prosecco aperitif, just like last time?" could be a risky question if the customer is visiting for the first time with their spouse. In short, personalization and customization must serve the customer's interests and not harm them!

This might be obvious, but it's better not left unsaid: discretion is extremely important. Customer data must never be shared with any third parties. Aside from meeting the legal requirements, recording customer data serves only one purpose: providing the demanding customer with superior service.

1. **Not personalizing your service is appropriate for customers who do not want it**
2. **Be cautious about sharing information with colleagues**
3. **Reason from the customer's perspective. What would they consider appropriate?**
4. **Determine in each situation whether the use of certain information is appropriate**
5. **Discretion: never share customer information with other organizations**

8.5. LEGAL RESTRICTIONS

There are also legal restrictions to consider. The EU-level GDPR (General Data Protection Regulation) went into effect on 25 May 2018. Aimed at protecting privacy, it strictly limits the recording and storing of personal data. It is important for you to understand and comply with this legislation, as not doing so can result in fines of up to 20 million euros.

1. **Your organization must comply with the GDPR or other privacy laws in your country**
2. **This restricts which customer data you can record and keep**

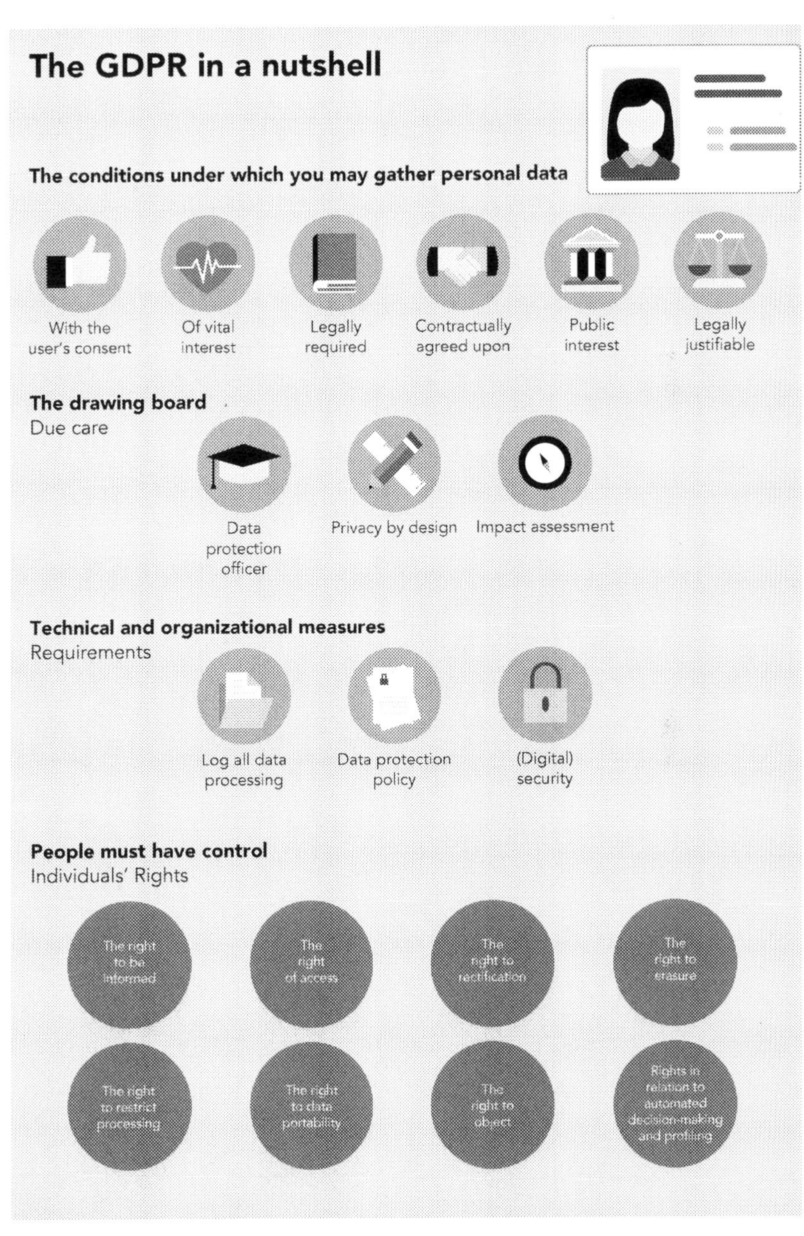
The GDPR in a nutshell
The conditions under which you may gather personal data
With the user's consent
Of vital interest
Legally required
Contractually agreed upon
Public interest
Legally justifiable
The drawing board
Due care
Data protection officer
Privacy by design
Impact assessment
Technical and organizational measures
Requirements
Log all data processing
Data protection policy
(Digital) security
People must have control
Individuals' Rights
The right to be informed
The right of access
The right to rectification
The right to erasure
The right to restrict processing
The right to data portability
The right to object
Rights in relation to automated decision-making and profiling

FIGURE 18. The GDPR in a Nutshell[22]

RULE 4

We collect and use customer data in order to provide customized service, but in doing so we must comply with legal requirements. Therefore, always check whether what you intend to do is legally permitted. The customer must be asked for and give consent (crucial point) before you may enter and store any of their personal data. The customer must also have the opportunity to view and correct these data.
Does your organization keep personal data? Then it must carefully protect this data. In terms of privacy policy, keep these points in mind:

- Your organization is not allowed not keep more personal data than is strictly necessary.
- Your organization must ensure that access to these data is restricted to those who need access.
- Your organization may be required under the GDPR to carry out a Data Protection Impact Assessment (DPIA). This is an extensive audit into the risks in your organization's data processes. This might mean your organization will be required to take measures to minimize these risks.
- There are limits to how long your organization may keep data, namely only as long as strictly necessary.
- Always check what legislation applies in your country; in the EU, the GDPR applies, other legislation may apply where you work.

8.6. IN SHORT

Demanding customers expect you to remember them and their preferences so that you can offer them tailored service. This gives them the feeling they are valued as a customer, important, and not just a number. By structurally noting down information from the contact history, explicit & implicit signals and other information about the customer from the public domain, you can create a good profile of the customer, their previous encounters with the organization, preferences, family situation, and so on. By applying this information appropriately during contacts with the customer, you can even give demanding customers World-Class Service. But keep in mind that there are limits to what you can do. Some customers don't want personalized service. Also, your use of personal information must be in the customer's interest. In some situations, it is not a good idea to personalize your service because it might embarrass the customer. Finally, laws and regulations restrict how you can use personal data.

REALITY CHECK

- Do you use your personal antennae to pick up relevant customer information?
- Do you record and keep this information? Why (or why not)?
- Do you use the available customer information to offer customers personalized service?
- Do you always ask yourself whether offering personalized service is in your customer's interest?
- Do you comply with the GDPR or other regulations in force?

READ MORE

Ultimate GDPR Practitioner Guide
Stephen Robert Massey – ISBN 9781999827236

The GDPR Challenge
Amie Taal – ISBN 9780367257262

(US)
Federal Trade Commission Privacy Law and Policy
Chris Jay Hoofnagle – ISBN 978-1107126787

9

WOW THE CUSTOMER

9.1. INTRODUCTION

The fifth rule we will discuss is: wow your customers by thrilling them, surprising them, and exceeding their expectations a little or a lot. Referring back to the three groups of expectation factors in the Kano model (dissatisfiers, satisfiers and delighters, see Fig. 1) wowing your customers means doing better than expected on the satisfiers (exceeding expectations). But it also means going above and beyond any expectations by doing something that the customer could not have imagined.

Some organizations tell their customer service reps to turn every encounter with their customers into a wow experience. This leads to the reps bending over backwards in a forced way, anything to wow the customer. Or, wowing the customer becomes a sad routine that has nothing to do with offering World-Class Service and an extraordinary customer experience. In fact, we think it would be quite an achievement if every employee managed to wow one customer a day. Don't turn this into a standard 'trick', just use your instinct to give the right customer at the right time this feeling. What works for one customer, doesn't work for another. Use your own judgment, and trust yourself. Besides, customers can tell when they're being given special treatment. Don't let an extraordinary experience get watered down into an obligatory gesture. If it feels fake to the customer, it's going to backfire on you big time.

Wowing the customer also doesn't work if they feel that the basics are not covered (Rules 1 and 2). This means that if your organization still has work to do in those areas, you shouldn't be putting too much time and energy into trying to go above and beyond. Just get the basics down pat first. And keep the Excellence Paradox in mind. If you and your organization continually strive to offer excellent service, that level of service will soon come to be seen as standard by customers. Remember, the delighters and extraordinary customer experiences of today are the dissatisfiers of tomorrow!

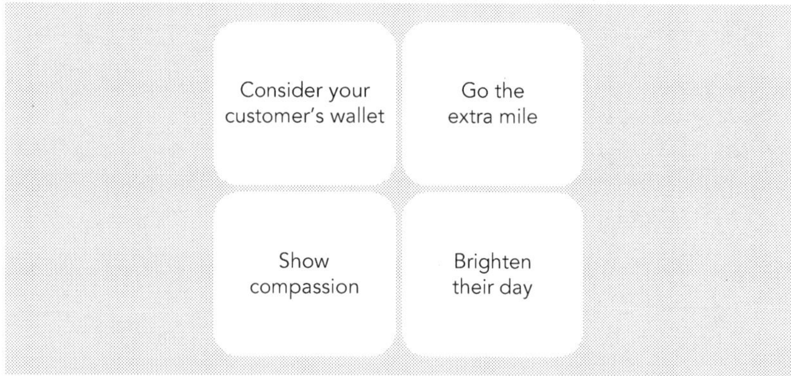

FIGURE 19. The Four Aspects of Rule 5, Wow the Customer

In the sections below, we will describe four sources of inspiration for finding wow-moments. Often, this has to do with special or emotional moments for customers in which you can make a difference. We will also discuss a fifth aspect of this, the Service Recovery Paradox, in Chapter 10. Look for the right moments, find them, and use them to make an unforgettable impression. The beautiful thing is that your own intuition, your own sixth sense, is a perfect guide to follow in this respect. You really do feel when the moment is right.

9.2. CONSIDER YOUR CUSTOMER'S WALLET

When a customer orders a bottle of white wine priced at 50 euros, the sommelier points out that there's another wine on the list that matches the food better and only costs 30 euros. A mechanic at an auto repair shop tells the customer they may as well order an overhauled auto part instead of a new one because it's just as good and will save them hundreds of euros. An air conditioning salesperson tells the customer that the most expensive model is far too heavy duty for the living room in their home. In all three of these examples, the organization is taking the customer's wallet into account. The priority is not the short-term profit, but honest product advice and the long-term relationship with the customer.

1. **Don't squeeze your customer dry**
2. **The long-term relationship with customers is more important than short-term profit**

9.3. GO THE EXTRA MILE

A lease car customer brings a damaged vehicle to the repair shop. The lease contract says the customer gets to borrow a small replacement car. Problem is, the customer is about to go on vacation with the whole family, including three kids. They'll never fit in the economy class car they have a right to under the lease. A lease company employee hears about this and takes immediate action, ordering a bigger replacement vehicle and a fun travel kit for the kids. The car is waiting outside the family's home on the morning of their departure.

A family's Christmas tree falls over just three days before Christmas, destroying the exclusive ornaments from Christel Dauwe in Antwerp. One phone call is enough to solve the problem. A replacement set of ornaments is sent by courier to Rotterdam that very day. Payment can wait. What matters is that there is a beautifully decorated tree in time for Christmas.

A car dealership's VIP customer is on vacation, a 10-hour flight from home. The dealer wants to give the customer the opportunity to try out the latest model for the weekend. Not at home, but at his holiday destination. It's not easy to arrange, but the dealer gets it done. When the customer checks in at his hotel and asks to rent a car, the receptionist tells him there's a car waiting for him: not a rental but a cost-free car for the weekend, and the newest model there is.

These are three examples of 'going the extra mile': putting in that extra effort that goes way beyond the standard things you do to serve a customer. You work a few hours extra, take the long way, do something that actually has nothing to do with your normal product or service, all to wow the customer.

You put lots of energy into something special for the customer, arranging the unexpected. This often-used method for wowing the customer consists of extreme helpfulness, and not only when the customer has a problem (see next Rule).

1. **Go the extra mile for the customer**
2. **Do this without expecting anything in return**

9.4. SHOW COMPASSION

Sometimes, your organization's rules and procedures stand in the way of you offering World-Class Service. You want to serve the customer, but the rules don't allow it. The customer might need to withdraw money because of serious financial problems, but under normal procedure, they can only withdraw from the account three months from now. Or perhaps your customer wants to install the electronic equipment you sold him in his home, but he can't because he's confined to a wheelchair. "Can't we make an exception to the rule that we don't provide at-home service after 5 p.m.? After all, it's only four minutes past five!" And here's an even better (or worse) example: "The kitchen closes at 11 p.m. It's now 10:55. Sorry, we can't serve you anymore. Better luck next time!"

Remember the rule of hard and soft rules. The hard rules are etched in stone. They are based on laws and other weighty considerations. Those are the rules you can't bend. But many organizations also have a big grey area of rules they can bend if it benefits the customer and doesn't cause any major problems. If you can help a customer out by bending those rules, then just do it. Do explain it to your boss later on, of course. Show compassion and make exceptions if it makes a big difference to the customer. It's also important to show the customer that you are willing to make an exception but that this is not normally done. This prevents the customer from drawing the conclusion that the extra effort you are putting in is nothing special. The exception you make today must not set a precedent that raises expectations of your standard service level.

1. **Know the hard and soft rules in your organization**
2. **Bend the soft rules whenever you feel it's doable and benefits the customer (compassion)**

9.5. BRIGHTEN YOUR CUSTOMER'S DAY

There are two ways to brighten your customer's day: small acts of kindness and celebrating special moments. The most common type of surprise is probably a small act of kindness, which is really a way to show your customer that you are thinking of them. A German hotel located on 'Unterschweinstiege' – Lower Pig Alley – sells little wooden pigs as a souvenir. They're a funny reference to the local livestock. Guests can buy one for a few euros. When a particular guest is checking out and asks for two pigs for his daughter, he's told he can have them for free. "They're so cute, aren't they? Here you go, a small gift from us to you, Mr Peters." It's just a small gesture, but it is attentive, and brightens Mr Peters' day.

Many organizations make use of such small gestures in their daily dealings with customers. One body repair shop gives customers a scale model of a Mini Cooper when handing back the keys to their repaired car. Nespresso sends small gift box of coffee pods to its customers once a year. Upscale hotels leave a nice holiday gift in the rooms of their regular guests. Nearly every beauty shop gives out small samples of lotions and perfumes for customers to try out (and really good sales people are selective about what they give out, trying to make an educated guess of what each customer is likely to appreciate). Many offices give out goody bags to clients when they leave the building. Yes, these are small gestures. Not to compensate for something that's gone wrong, but to put the cherry on the cake.

We would like to add a few tips here. In some cases, these little gestures become so standard that the element of surprise is gone. Gifts work best when there is something authentic about them, like the wooden piglets at the hotel. They have a connection to the local folklore. Another example is the tool seller who gives away little wrenches that can be used as letter openers. Both of these examples are fun, unique and specific. Another tip is to make sure you never give a customer the same gift more than once. If you give a customer a reusable water bottle for the third time when they visit your organization, it will start to wear thin. All things considered, it's the custom acts of kindness (small gifts that suit the customer's interests and hobbies) that are most effective.

1. **Does your organization show 'small acts of kindness'? If so, use them actively**
2. **Know your customers' important and special moments**
3. **Brighten their day on these occasions**

Another way to brighten your customer's day is when you pay attention to the special moments in their lives. Maybe it's their birthday, or an anniversary. Maybe one of them has just become a grandparent. Or they've been your customer for ten years. Keep an eye on these dates, track them and use them to show your customer that you're thinking of them, that they're important to you. Make their special moments even more special, so that even demanding customers will remember. Like the way every KLM plane has a few little gifts on board to give away to kids who are celebrating their birthday on the day of their flight. Restaurants do the same: they serve an extra special dessert when it happens to be one of their guests' birthday. No matter what organization you work for, you can always find a way to show you care about the special moments in a customer's life, whatever those moments are.

Some customers find it a really big moment when they've just bought a car. If you're a car salesperson, you might not see that as such a big deal, because you close several deals in a single day. But put yourself in the customer's shoes, and make it a great experience. When one buyer purchased an expensive German car for a few hundred thousand euros, the dealer had thought ahead. He knew the customer was going to bring his son along to pick up the car, so when they arrived he had a surprise ready: two objects hidden under a silk sheet. Next to the luxury automobile, there was a little pedal car of the same model. The father was so thrilled, he almost forgot about the car he bought. For other customers, the special moment might be a very different one. There's the story of the little kid who twisted his ankle when he fell at the zoo. By responding quickly, taking care of the child, giving him a stuffed animal and offering the family a free meal before helping them continue their visit to the zoo, the employees made sure it was still a great family outing. And remember Joshie, the lost giraffe (see Section 2.4).

9.6. IN SHORT

Wowing your customers by slightly exceeding or going way beyond expectations can have a particularly positive effect on demanding customers. But watch out: some customers are already so used to special treatment that they see it as a basic service that they have a right to expect. Nevertheless, there are four ways to wow your customer. Considering your customer's wallet, going the extra mile, making an exception to the rule where you can, and brightening their day by showing them a small act of kindness, or celebrating their special occasions.

REALITY CHECK

- Do you ever wow your customers? How often? One customer per day?
- Do you try to get your customers to spend the maximum, or do you take their wallet into account?
- Are there moments when you go the extra mile to help the customer out?
- Do you make exceptions for your customers (out of compassion) when your organization's rules can be bent? Can you name three recent examples?
- Do you regularly brighten your customers' day? By giving them a small gift, for instance, or by marking a special day in their life?

The Paradox of Excellence
David Mosby & Michael Weissman – ISBN 9780787981396

De Customer Delight Strategie
Jean-Pierre Thomassen – ISBN 9789013110159
(highly recommended but available in Dutch only)

Service Excellence – Principles and Model
International standards ISO 23592

Customer Delight
Alain Guillemain – ISBN 9780985585907

10 USE THE SERVICE RECOVERY PARADOX

10.1. INTRODUCTION

A group of friends had decided to take a road trip. All of them run their own businesses, and all of them have busy lives, but they share a passion: cars. They've carefully planned the trip and rented out a French castle to enjoy French cuisine, fine wines and cognac. Their daytime activities will revolve around cars. But then, on Friday afternoon, the main organizer discovers an embarrassing problem. He's recently bought a new car, but now he's having mechanical problems. He won't be able to take part in the great tours planned for the weekend. Not pleased with this situation (partly because of the snide jokes from his friends about his new lemon), he calls his dealer. As you can probably imagine, it was a challenge to help the man out on a Friday afternoon in another country. The dealer calls the manufacturer. That same afternoon, an employee from the carmaker drives to the castle in France with a bag of tools and some spare parts. At 1 a.m., using an iPhone light and a flashlight, the guy starts doing repairs.

The following morning, the car owner walks outside to find a note on his car, which reads: "Have a great drive today." After having disappointed the customer because his brand-new car broke down, the manufacturer earned back the customer's respect by showing so much dedication. By driving down to France and fixing the car, he made sure not only his customer, but also the customer's friends, had a great experience in France.

'Clients will always remember a negative experience no matter how many positive moments have been shared.'[23] Negative experiences always stick with the customer. The upside is this: if ever there was a single moment when you could make a difference between average service and World-Class Service, a moment when you can wow your customer, then this is it: when the customer lets you know they have a problem. In situations like this, customers' emotions can run high and their reactions are likely to be magnified. This can be positive or negative, depending on how you respond. Emotions can be a catalyst.

That's why it's so important to create a positive experience in response to a negative one. This keeps customers loyal. It's called Service Recovery. It means correcting below-par service in order to win back a potentially lost customer. The Service Recovery Paradox has to do with the quality of the repair. When a customer's problem is solved in an exceptionally positive way, this tends to make the customer even more appreciative than when they've never had a problem in the first place (see Fig. 20). A great solution strengthens the customer's trust in your organization.

In this sixth rule, we discuss the importance of picking up on relevant clues from customers and taking ownership of the problems they present. In addition to reading these clues and being proactive, there are problems customers communicate

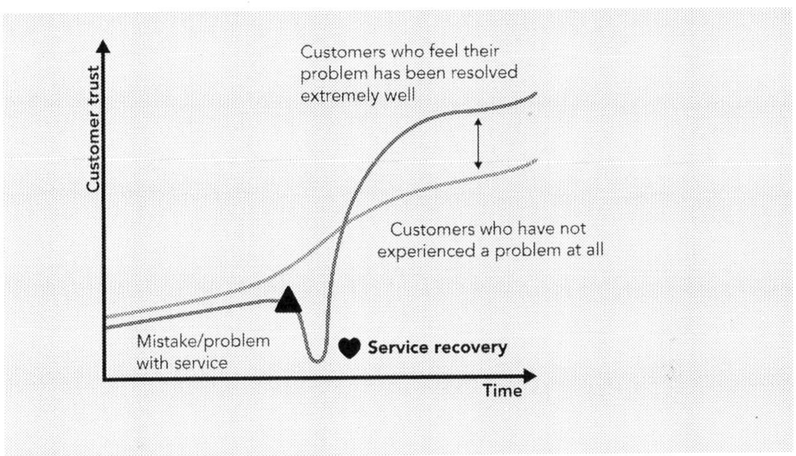

FIGURE 20. The Service Recovery Paradox

to you in comments, suggestions, requests for help and even complaints. Ways to respond to these problems will be discussed in Section 10.3. Next, we'll deal with the fact that demanding customers don't take no for an answer. And finally, we will look at how you can exceed customer expectations in service recovery, in order to use the paradox in your favor.

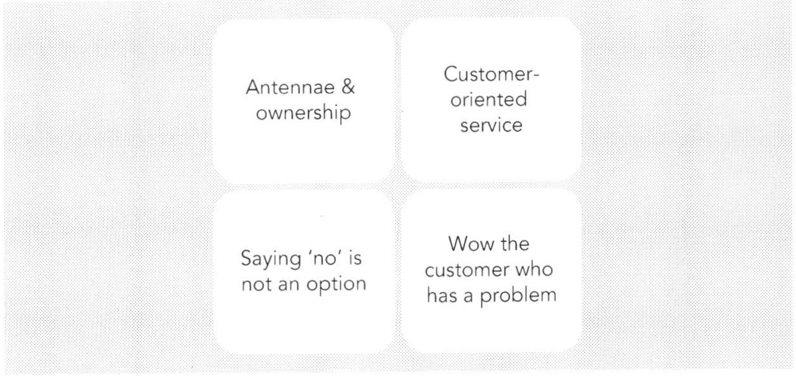

FIGURE 21. The Four Aspects of Rule 6, Use the Service Recovery Paradox

10.2. ANTENNAE & OWNERSHIP

You might have dozens or even hundreds of contacts with customers every day. Most are routine contacts, but some of your customers are experiencing problems. Maybe a product isn't working, or they don't understand how to get it working. They might have made a mistake themself, but whatever it is, things aren't going smoothly, and the customer has a problem. Customers don't always take the time to tell you this. Instead of formally complaining, they just distract themselves with something else. That may have something to do with the culture, the specific industry you work in, or the type of customer they are, but the fact is, not everyone who has a problem or is dissatisfied actually tells the company responsible. Depending on which industry we're talking about, only between 10 and 50% of dissatisfied customers let you know about it. Why do so many people not complain? Is it too difficult? Are people not aware that they have a right to complain? Do they not have faith that something will be done about it? Do they worry that complaining might be used against them later?

This is why it's so key for customer service reps to develop their antennae and learn to read the clues customers give. There are in fact three types of signals: non-signals, implicit signals and explicit signals. It's a non-signal when a customer doesn't let anyone know there's a problem, but you know it anyway from experience or because your systems tell you so. Perhaps you get an error message, or you see from the contact history that there's something wrong, that the customer is having difficulty navigating the portal, and so on. The customer is not sending a signal, but you're getting one anyway. When the customer is not saying straightforwardly that there is a problem, but you pick up on the fact that things have gone awry from what they <u>do</u> say, it's an implicit signal. You might be able to read the implicit complaint in certain comments, questions or suggestions, for instance. Non-verbal signals are part of this category, such as a customer drumming their fingers on the information desk, or the use of phrases like "late," "not yet," "again." These indicate a problem in a roundabout way, as do comments from customers on surveys. The explicit signals are the obvious ones, the complaints about things like products that don't work and expressions of dissatisfaction with the organization. You probably encounter several such signals of all types every day, which is why good antennae are key. There's a saying that every complaint is an opportunity. We'd like to widen that: every *signal* is an opportunity. Every signal is a chance to make a difference by putting the Service Recovery Paradox to work.

Ever heard the bicycle tire story? A customer goes to the bike shop to return a new tire. His wife had bought the wrong size. The employee takes the wrong tire back and asks the customer to come back in a few days, when the right size tire will be back in stock. A few days later, the customer is at the shop again to say he's made a mistake. This wasn't the shop where is wife had bought the tire. The employee nods because he knows this already, and says he has the right tire for him now anyway. This is a great example of an employee who didn't have to help the customer but did anyway. He did not waste any unnecessary energy on investigating whether the complaint was well-founded; he focused on finding a solution for the customer. The assumption underlying this behavior is simple: 'It's not always our fault, but it's always our problem.' See the customer's problem, regardless of whether it was caused by you, a co-worker, your organization's IT system, another organization, or the customer themself, as a chance to turn the customer into a fan.

We know from experience that the practice described above is the best recipe for satisfaction. There are situations where customers have a problem or complaint that is their own fault. The key is to solve these problems anyway and, in so doing, to exceed the customer's expectations. It bears repeating that this is the best way to make your customer a fan. We see in this situation that the more emotional a customer is, the more extreme their reaction when they get World-Class Service and their problem is solved.

Some customers have been known to send written compliments, cakes, and flowers, and to write great reviews on social media. They've even gone so far as to nominate organizations for a prize on consumer programs on TV. It doesn't get any better than that.

1. **'Antennae out' for implicit & explicit signals and signals the customer isn't even sending**
2. **Unfounded complaints don't exist**
3. **It's not always your fault, but it's always your problem**

What if you're not on the lookout for possible problems? What if you don't assume ownership? That can trigger the rule of exponential damage. Imagine you are a computer manufacturer. If a faulty microchip is discovered during manufacturing, it might cost 1 euro to replace it. If the chip is already on a PCB, replacing it costs 10 euros. If you don't solve the problem until the computer is assembled, replacing the chip will cost 100 euros. And if the problem doesn't get tackled until a customer realizes they have a malfunctioning computer (because of the faulty microchip), the costs of repair will run up to 1,000 euros. In short, the sooner you detect and resolve a problem, the smaller the damage will be. The same goes for service recovery. A comment that is ignored might evolve into a formal complaint, a complaint that isn't handled could become a claim, and before you know it, your superior could find themself in court.

10.3. CUSTOMER-ORIENTED SERVICE

As a service representative, you can make or break your organization's relationship with the customer, all the more so when dealing with complaints. Many organizations score just 3 points out of 5 from customers when it comes to how they deal with the signals that something's not right. Not so much because customers don't get what they want, but mainly because of how service reps communicate. Customers report that reps tend not to really listen, so customers feel they are not taken seriously and they have to settle for a solution that doesn't fully address the problem. To prevent this, it's a good idea to structure your communication with customers into five steps. These are the same steps that are taught by service training agencies. Applying them boosts customer satisfaction. The main idea is to focus on the customer, not the signal, because one and the same signal can mean something very different to different customers. Take lost luggage, for instance. If a traveler discovers at the airport that a piece of luggage is missing, this seems like a pretty standard problem that can be dealt with according to the standard lost luggage procedure. But a lost suitcase full of dirty laundry probably means something very different to a traveler than a bag full of memorabilia of a recently deceased spouse. This is why it is so important to focus on the customer and to look for the deeper problem underlying the surface problem.

Step 1: Listen

When a customer sends a signal, listen. Take the time to really understand the customer. After all, there is a big difference between hearing and listening. If you're in a noisy space, look for a quieter place to talk. If you don't have much time, rearrange your schedule so that you do. Take notes and show the customer that you are actively listening. Nod and voice your understanding ('uh-huh') out loud. But try not to interrupt the customer during this first step. Don't assume that you already understand the problem, because the average complaint doesn't exist. Active listening gives the customer a chance to blow off steam and gives you time to prepare for the following step.

Step 2: Show Empathy

After listening, show some understanding. Let the customer know you see the problem and are also unhappy with the situation they are in. Apologize on behalf of your organization. Show that you get it and say you're sorry for the inconvenience. That's not the same as taking the blame. But showing empathy makes the customer feel they're being taken seriously. There is a difference here between sympathy and empathy. By showing sympathy, you run the risk of putting down your own organization. Avoid this at all times. By showing empathy, you run no such risk. Empathy is your personal capacity to put yourself into someone else's shoes.

Step 3: Get to the Bottom of Things

In this step, you complete the Listen-Summarize-Dig deeper circle (aka LSD). You ask more questions in order to understand the deeper underlying problem. And by asking the right questions, you get a picture of the possible avenues you could take to find a solution. Summarize the problem as you understand it and check with the customer whether you have understood it correctly. It can't hurt at this stage to ask the customer what kind of solution

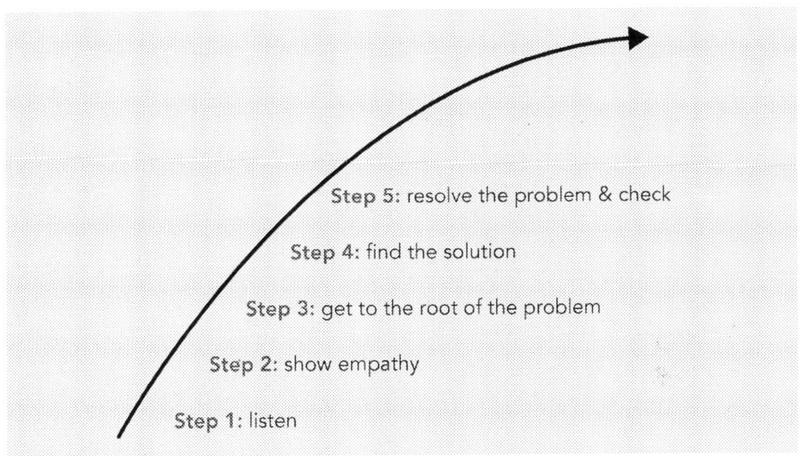

FIGURE 22. The 5-step Problem-Solving Method

they are looking for. What is the main reason for your complaint and how can we help solve the problem for you? You might find, for instance, that clients in the care sector tend to complain because they want to ensure that what happened to them doesn't happen to anyone else. In this case, someone is not hoping for financial compensation but merely want to see that you and your organization are learning something from the situation so that it does not repeat itself.

Step 4: Find a Solution

Based on what you have heard, you can now propose two or three solutions to the customer. "We can do A, which has these pros and cons, but we can also do B, which has these pros and cons." Only offer options that are feasible, of course. And consider the soft and hard rules (see Section 9.4). Hard rules are unbreakable, but soft ones can be bent. By letting the customer choose the solution, you are also giving them a feeling of sharing responsibility. This has a strongly positive effect on the satisfaction the customer will take away from this incident. Separate the solution: "Would this be a good solution for you?" or "Which of these solutions do you prefer, or do you see another possibility?" In the end, you choose a solution together. Work out the details together and make clear agreements on how to proceed. Conclude this step by thanking the customer. Keep in mind that they have given you the opportunity to solve the problem, while they could have just turned their back on you and your organization.

Step 5: Resolve the Problem & Follow Up
A deal is a deal, so whatever it is you agreed with the customer, you now have to stick to that 100%. If it is something you yourself can do, it's simple. If you need your co-workers or even other departments to step up, it can get more complicated. Be sure to remain the owner of the problem in all communications with the customer. Check to make sure your organization keeps the deal you made with the customer. Nothing would be worse than failing to do this. Then, follow up and check whether the customer is entirely satisfied with the solution. Only when the customer has confirmed this, can you close the case.

1. **Focus on the customer, not the signal. Uncover the underlying problem**
2. **Apply the five steps consistently**
3. **Close the case only when the customer has expressed satisfaction with the solution as executed**

10.4. SAYING NO IS NOT AN OPTION

Many organizations find it okay to say no to some customers. Their point is that saying no can be clear answer to unreasonable demands, especially if it goes against the organization's rules or guidelines. In these organizations, service representatives will say things like "we don't do that," or "we can't offer that level of service," or "that's not our policy," and so on. The problem is, demanding customers don't want to hear those excuses. A simple no can provoke or even enrage them. They are not used to being contradicted and are certainly not going to accept walking away empty-handed. Maybe you're thinking: 'those customers just have to get used to it' or 'well then take your business somewhere else,' but surely you understand that this is not an option. Instead, try to see it as a challenge. That doesn't mean you always have to say yes and cave in to the customer. But it does mean that you do everything in your power to avoid saying no by looking at what is possible. Another way of putting this is: be creative and think out of the box when looking for a solution to a problem.

1. **Find a way to avoid saying 'no'**
2. **Be creative in seeking solutions**
3. **There are limits, don't cave in to the customer**

We are not saying that you should do absolutely everything the customer demands. There are limits, of course. The customer's interests must also be weighed up against the organization's long-term interests. But every time you offer a creative solution and don't tell your customer 'no,' you have made a difference.

10.5. WOW THE CUSTOMER WHO HAS A PROBLEM

The way to put the Service Recovery Paradox to work for you is to pick up on the signals your customer sends out and show ownership, to follow the five steps in dealing with the problem, in avoiding saying no and, on top of all this, finding a way to wow the customer if you can. Some organizations – hopefully yours too – strive to leave customers deeply satisfied, or better yet, fans. To wow these customers, you're going to have to exceed their expectations, to go above and beyond their demands. That means going the extra mile and dealing with the problem better, quicker, more conveniently and with more of a personal touch. In other words, your baseline is not what the customer expects, but what the customer hopes for, or even more than that.

1. **Go above and beyond what the customer expects**
2. **Solve the problem better, faster, more conveniently and more personally than expected**
3. **Give the customer something extra as a gesture of your appreciation.**

In our home country, the Netherlands, there is a consumer affairs show on TV that gives awards to businesses for providing excellent service. Usually, the winning organizations have done something to wow the customer, and the customer has in turn sent a glowing commendation to the consumer show. What is interesting is that in most of these cases, the organization turned a problem into an opportunity to wow the customer. More often than not, the situation was caused by the customer's own mistake or by some other organization. And yet, the winners generously and compassionately solve the problem anyway. They focus on the customer and they find a solution. So, the business owner personally delivers the missing parts, or asks an employee to jump in the car and drive clear across the country to make sure that wedding ring is there on time for the ceremony. And to top off this faster, easier, better, and more personal-than-expected solution, the customer also gets a little gift of appreciation. A bunch of flowers, a bottle of wine, or another present that's suitable to the organization you work for.

10.6. IN SHORT

The Service Recovery Paradox is about providing customers with such a good response to their problem or complaint that they end up even more satisfied than they would have been if they never had a problem in the first place. To achieve this effect, you need good antennae for possible problems and a sense for when there is a chance to shine. The signals customers send can be implicit or explicit, or even non-existent (but you can tell from the contact history things haven't gone smoothly, for instance). If you are on the lookout, you can spot an opportunity to turn a problem into an opportunity to wow your customer. Take ownership, even if the problem is not your fault. By focusing on the customer and not the problem and dealing with the complaint in five steps, you can enlist the customer's help in finding a good, satisfying solution. Avoid saying no and look for a creative solution, because we all know demanding customers don't take no for an answer. Add a little something extra in the mix and solve the problem faster or better than expected, or offer a small gift afterwards, and you will have a new fan.

REALITY CHECK

- How good are you at reading customers' signals? How sensitive are your antennae?
- Do you see signals as opportunities? Do you focus on the customer (instead of the signal)?
- How skilled are you at the five steps?
- How often do you say no? Could you find more creative solutions instead?
- What do you do to exceed the expectations of customers with a problem?

READ MORE

YES! Attitude
Jeffrey Gitomer – ISBN 9780999255506

YES is the Answer! What is the Question?
Cameron Mitchell – ISBN 9781940858715

PART C

WHAT DEMANDS
DOES THIS PLACE
ON YOUR EMPLOYER?

11 PRECONDITIONS FOR WORLD-CLASS SERVICE

11.1. INTRODUCTION

In Part A of this book, we sketched the setting and context in which you work on offering World-Class Service. There, and in the six rules we discussed in Part B, we described what this requires of you. Like we said: it requires Olympic-level performance. To do it right, you need to be sharp, alert, creative, have an eye for detail, and be able to put the customer first. But just like any Olympic athlete, you can only succeed if certain preconditions are met. If you work in an organization that values excellent service, it's up to you to help keep these preconditions in place and improve them wherever possible. Tell your superiors what you need to be able to deliver that World-Class Service. If you are just starting out at an organization, try to find out to what extent these preconditions are already in place.

In this chapter, we go into five of these preconditions: sustainable ambitions, inspiring leadership, the right team, room to make your own decisions and continuous development and improvement. Each of the following sections discusses one of these preconditions. There are certainly more preconditions than the ones we talk about here, but we have limited ourselves to this key set of five.

11.2. A STEADY COURSE

A big accountancy firm came up with a new mission statement in which it emphasized the goal of offering customers an extraordinary experience and turning them into fans. The mission statement was launched at a quarterly meeting of all employees. There were breakout sessions of smaller groups to discuss the implications. A booklet was printed and sent to the home of each employee. A celebrity had been invited to give a speech. It looked like the company was really going to focus on the customer. However, nine months later, hardly anything had changed. The firm's ambition was never talked about anymore, and the only thing managers seemed interested in was how many billable hours the accountants could claim. Clearly, this is not the idea.

It is reasonable to expect the organization you work for to map out a clear strategy aimed at offering World-Class Service and a great customer experience, in which demanding customers are treated as a welcome challenge, not a burden. If you break it down further, what the organization needs is actually three things: a clear, ambitious strategy, a way to turn their good intentions into action, and staying power, or a stable course.

A clear and ambitious strategy expresses what the organization wants to do for its customers. It defines the ideal customer experience, the organization's higher purpose, what customers can expect, what this means for the organization and what goals and objectives the organization attaches to this.

Organizations that really want to make a difference for their customers make this explicit in the organization's vision, mission statement, policy documents and annual plans. Usually, managers have involved both employees and customers in this process. If you work for an organization like this, or are applying for a job at one, ask to see these documents.

Many organizations manage to do it on paper, like the accountancy firm we just talked about. But the proof of the pudding is in the eating. In the end, the only thing that matters is what organizations do in practice. Do they only talk the talk, or do they also walk the walk? Do they put time, money and effort into organizing and offering World-Class Service? Are customer satisfaction and experience a top priority, or at least a key performance indicator? Are they metrics that are tracked and that you, as an employee, are held accountable for? Or is your organization actually only interested in sales, costs, productivity and profit?

Do you and your team have enough time to offer customers World-Class Service? You can only make a difference if your organization takes actions that match its words. Pay attention to the following indicators:

- What is the main focus when new employees are onboarded? What is the core message they are given?
- What is the focus of most of the training offered to employees? What are the most important topics?
- What do managers and company executives lose sleep over? What issues are at the top of the management agenda?
- What metrics do managers use to track results? What performance indicators are bonuses based on?
- What does the CEO focus on in their speeches to employees and staff?

If the answer to all these questions is "the customer," you are probably in a good place. If the answer is: "sales, costs, productivity and profit," what is your conclusion?

Providing World-Class Service is only possible if your organization charts a course and sticks to it. It's no good to have a "Year of the Customer" one year, but to go straight back to cost-cutting and stripping down service the next. Building up a team of dedicated service employees requires years of work. An organization that excels at breaking things down never manages to build anything. Is your organization a construction business or actually more of a demolition business? Successful organizations with a lasting reputation for World-Class Service have achieved this by pursuing a steady course. Often, this is in the organization's DNA. It's not a project, but a habit.

11.3. INSPIRING LEADERSHIP

A director of a large business that runs holiday cabin parks likes being amidst the employees, not in the boardroom or at the computer looking at spread sheets. The director is often seen in the customer service center, talking to employees about what they're hearing from the clientele, or listening in to customer service phone calls. Every week, the director personally handles a handful of complaints. Several times a year, he visits every cabin park. And there, too, he walks around and works side by side with the employees. The point is to hear what they need to provide World-Class Service every day. The director wants the employees to experience the company management as supportive, not as a nuisance. At the same time, he takes every opportunity to stress the importance of creating happy customers. Employees and customers are the central focus at all times: during meetings, on the intranet and during working breakfasts with employees.

World-Class Service starts at the top. Managers and board members have a lot of influence on the culture in an organization. They determine what is acceptable and what isn't. They are the ambassadors and change agents that help the organization to change course, but also to stay the course once a new one has been set. From experience we know that a new director or management can give an organization renewed momentum. What they do and don't do, say and don't say has great impact on the organization and all its employees. Do they set the right example and show that providing World-Class Service is a priority? Do they inspire people, do they provide the preconditions needed? Are they close to the employees and customers? These are all important factors. What's it like in your organization? Do you feel inspired to provide World-Class Service, even to the most demanding customers?

Does the organization see you as an asset, a valuable team member who contributes to the success of the organization? Or does it treat you like a cog in a machine, a replaceable part that just costs money? We think this is an important question when it comes to the key issue of inspiring leadership. Things can only work if management and board believe that employees really do make all the difference between adequate service and World-Class Service. If they're willing to invest in the long-term relationship with employees, and in growth and quality, then there's a sound basis to work on providing World-Class Service. Does your organization meet this description?

> *I am a man of simple tastes; I am easily satisfied with the best*
>
> **WINSTON CHURCHILL**

11.4. THE RIGHT TEAM

The Formula One driver pulls in. The pit crew know exactly what to do, and exactly 1.82 seconds later the car is back on the track, refueled and with four new tires. It's astounding how much time, procedure, instruction, training, material and preparation it takes to be able to achieve this. Of course, Max Verstappen ends up on the winner's stage. Wow! But behind his great effort are about 800 people who are celebrating, too. They win as a team. The driver is the most visible hero, but every individual on that team is important. Every one of them contributes.

Providing World-Class Service and working according to the six rules outlined in this book, requires a team effort, too. You can't do it alone. That's why organizations have to build a team that can deliver that world-class performance. It all starts with hiring the right people and giving them the warm welcome they deserve. Just look at how Bentley onboards its new employees. Because new employees are given such a heartfelt welcome, they tend to be deeply committed to the brand and their work. The welcome is so extraordinary that it still brings a smile to their faces even after ten years on the job.

During the onboarding procedure, everything revolves around Bentley. The employees are picked up at the airport by chauffeur-driven Bentleys. The passion for the company is visible in the hotel where they stay, in the Bentley factory, and everywhere else they go. During the factory tour, a guide tells them that his cousin works in one department and his brother in another. It's truly a 'family' experience, with a sense of community, passion, a love of quality, and British hospitality and elegance. It's all any manager or CEO could ask for: employees who feel so much dedication and passion for the brand that they still speak lovingly about it even after they've been working there for decades.

When hiring people, it's important to look at their competences. But what's more crucial is attitude, motivation and passion. Competences can be learned, but the basic attitude, passion and enthusiasm (from the Greek ἔνθεος, entheos, which means "possessed by a god") are more deeply ingrained characteristics. Jim Collins talked about this in his bestseller *Good to Great*: first comes WHO, then WHAT. Do you have good people on your team? Do you work well together? Do you trust each other? Do you recognize each other's strengths and weaknesses? The best organizations have the best/right people in the right places.

11.5. ROOM TO MAKE DECISIONS

Is Mickey (read: a student in a Mickey Mouse costume) allowed to help a crying child at Disneyland get over their sadness about an ice cream cone that fell on the ground by taking the kid by the hand and cheerily skipping over to the ice cream parlor for a new cone? Maybe even letting the child scoop it themself? Or is that not allowed? Because it costs 2 euros and it takes time. Time that Mickey would otherwise have to wave at other children. Or it would set a precedent we want to avoid, because before you know it every kid will be dropping their cones on the ground.

An organization in the tourism industry has discarded many of the soft rules and procedures it had accumulated over the years. Not the hard and fast rules, of course, because they're based on laws. The company decided on this because employees had indicated that they felt the many rules prevented them from offering great service. The old guidelines, 20 pages long, were replaced by a single sheet of paper. The first and most important rule is "Use your common sense." The second is "Treat customers the way you would want to be treated."

Before this new set of rules took effect, employees had to ask their boss for permission every time they wanted to make an exception to a rule or authorize any financial decision in order to show leniency to a customer. That, too, was discarded, so employees can make these decisions on their own as long as their decision conforms to the basic rules on the new sheet. For expenditures under 500 euros, permission from their boss is no longer necessary.

Working in accordance with the six rules requires flexibility, creativity, an ability to react quickly to new situations and a willingness to customize service. After all, every customer is unique and every situation is different. And the last thing you need is a bunch of rules and guidelines, without being allowed to make any decisions. Demanding customers want you to act fast. Saying "I'll have to ask my boss first" doesn't go over well with them. Ritz Carlton employees are authorized to make big financial decisions when a customer deserves compensation because they've been inconvenienced for some reason. As it turns out, employees are very good at using this freedom responsibly. In the event that an employee makes a wrong decision that costs the company money, the employee is not punished for this. Mistakes aren't great, but people make mistakes. So be it, as long as they learn from them.

This is why it's so important for team leaders and managers to trust you and to have faith that you have the organization's best interests at heart and will not squander their money. It's also key that you get the room for maneuver and the stripes you need to do the right thing for the customer and the organization. You need room to be able to show compassion and bend the soft rules where necessary in order to serve the customer well and even wow them from time to time. Of course, it's good to discuss these things with your team afterwards. And it's also important that the number of rules is kept to a minimum and that there's a budget to pay for suitable solutions for the customer. Yes, it costs money, but that's the reality. You need to be able to send your customer a bunch of flowers on a big day for them, or better yet, send them a personalized gift. How is this organized in your organization? Do you get enough room to offer World-Class Service to demanding customers?

11.6. CONTINUOUS EDUCATION

No one can stay at the top of their game without training and education. Olympic athletes have to train every day, and the same goes for employees that want to deliver World-Class Service on a daily basis. You can't just rely on routines, on the assumption that you know what the customer wants because of earlier experiences, on a lazy idea like, "that's the way we do things here." Customers' expectations change over time and they usually grow. Today's delighter is tomorrow's dissatisfier. Continuous improvement is key. On the one hand, your employer must facilitate you and your team to make the most of your personal development. And on the other hand, you must be open to this and prepared to put in the work, because continuous education is your own responsibility.

Continuous improvement also means looking critically at yourself and how you handle encounters with customers. How did the customer respond? Did I respond to that in the right way? What could I have done better? By staying in Plan-Do-Check-Act mode, you learn from every encounter, every letter, every phone call, every flight, and so on. Use customer feedback – such as the results of continuous customer satisfaction surveys, complaints and other signals – to see what you can improve. Maybe it's a good idea to stop for a minute every day to consider what went well and what you really should keep doing, as well as what didn't go so well and what you will do differently from now on. Learning and developing on the job is probably 70% of all the improvement and development you need to make. It does help if your organization continues to provide fresh input by asking customers for feedback.

The other 30% of improvement and development comes from structured learning, through training, role play, mystery visits, feedback meetings and daily standups. These are activities your team leader or employer organizes and sets aside time for. Always take part in these and look at these activities as opportunities to gain new insight, learn new techniques and generally up your game.

11.7. IN SHORT

Working according to the six rules described in Part B is as tough as professional sports. It requires a lot of commitment from you. It also requires your team and organization to meet a number of preconditions so you can, and will want to, perform at the top of your game. We have selected the five most important preconditions: It's important that your organization has long-term, stable ambitions to provide World-Class Service and offer customers an extraordinary experience. Not only on paper but in practice, too. In addition, managers must motivate the rest of the organization through inspiring leadership and by hiring and maintaining a great team. Formula 1 drivers can't deliver their great performances without a fully-staffed, well-trained team behind them. The same goes for you. Also, in order to be flexible and provide tailored service, you need elbow room, so to speak. Room to decide, room to bend the rules, and room to spend money. And lastly, you need to keep getting better. Olympic athletes train every day. Likewise, your efforts to improve every day are a precondition to your organization's continued success. That's why your organization needs to facilitate you in this as much as possible.

REALITY CHECK

- Does your organization consistently work on delivering World-Class Service?
- Do your superiors inspire you and your co-workers to deliver World-Class Service?
- Do you work in a world-class team?
- Do you have enough room to serve customers according to the six rules?
- What do you do to continuously get better? What is your own role in this and how does your employer facilitate your efforts?

READ MORE

Management: Tasks, Responsibilities, Practices Peter Drucker – ISBN 9781138129467

Good to Great
Jim Collins – ISBN 9780066620992

The Basics of Hoshin Kanri
Randy K. Kesterson – ISBN 9781138438217

Customer Mania!
Ken Blanchard – ISBN 9780743270298

Service Excellence
Jean-Pierre Thomassen & Eric de Haan – ISBN 9789462760998
(highly recommended but available in Dutch only)

Excelleren in service
Jean-Pierre Thomassen & Eric de Haan – ISBN 9789462763425
(highly recommended but available in Dutch only)

ABOUT THE AUTHORS

Dennis Opstal got his degree in mechanical engineering and industrial engineering at West Brabant University of Applied Sciences in 1993. He has been working in the automotive industry since 1985. In 1995, he began working as an aftersales manager for an Italian motorcycle manufacturer.
Since 2006, he has been employed by one of the world's most prestigious hyper luxury carmakers, rising to the position of senior manager aftersales for Europe in 2018. Starting in 1995, he has worked ceaselessly to bring excellent service to various distribution networks. Opstal believes that both the customer experience and the organization's success depend on employees' motivation and continued education.
He has a life-long passion for service excellence and he is the MD of OCTS international B.V. Consultancy, supporting those that strive to deliver World-Class Service by joining the Service Excellence crusade (the never ending journey to improve your customers' experiences). He sees it as a daily challenge for businesses to provide excellent customer experiences, both to end users, co-workers and car dealerships, in all of Europe, and anywhere in the world where customers need service.

Since 1993, organizational consultant Jean-Pierre Thomassen has been helping organizations and their boards make the fundamental transition from inward-looking, product and process-focused operations to outward-focused, customer and service-oriented businesses. He is the chairman of the Dutch *Stichting Service Excellence*. He has written 15 books about customer service, including *Klanttevredenheid, de succesfactor voor elke organization* (1994), *Waardering door customers* (2002), *De Customer Delight Strategie* (2012) and, as co-author with Eric de Haan, *Service Excellence* (2015) and *Excelleren in service* (2019). In 2018, he earned his PhD with a thesis on service guarantees in the faculty of Economics and Business at the University of Groningen. Thomassen is also a lecturer at various institutes.

SOURCES & END NOTES

1 Source: https://www.fullsurge.com/blog/broken-promises-when-brands-dont-live-up-to-what-they-promised-to-deliver
2 This model was named after Professor Noriako Kano, who developed it in the 1980s to express the relationship between product characteristics and customer satisfaction.
3 Jan Carlzon (former CEO of SAS Scandinavian Airlines) originally called these 'Moments of Truth'.
4 Source: Shep Hyken.
5 See: De Customer Delight Strategie (Thomassen).
6 Source: Esteban Kolsky presenting his research (Thinkjar) during a presentation at the Callidus Customer Conference in Las Vegas 2013. CX for Executives (slideshare.net).
7 Source: TARP, Consumer Complaint Handling in America: Final Report, sponsored by the U.S. Office of Consumer Affairs, 1979.
8 Source: https://twitter.com/gitomer/status/245960871392710656?s=20&t=xzeDyoWH9RqD1-y13rFRow; and Jeffrey Gitomer Live - How to Not Suck at Sales (DVD)
9 See: Fred Wiersema - Customer Intimacy.
10 See: Diffusion of Innovation (DOI) Theory by E.M. Rogers
11 Source: De Customer Delight Strategie (Thomassen) p.47.
12 These levels are based on the Service Excellence Pyramid (see Service Excellence, Thomassen/De Haan and www.serviceexcellence.nu).
13 Source: Huffpost.com – Chris Hurn - Stuffed Giraffe Shows What Customer Service Is All About 05/17/2012.
14 Source: www.toolshero.nl

15 Source: https://www.toolshero.nl/psychologie/persoonlijkheidstypen/big-five-test/

16 Source: Janse, B. (2018). Big five test. Downloaded from Toolshero: https://www.toolshero.nl/psychologie/persoonlijkheidstypen/big-five-test/

17 Source: Earl Nightingale. The Strangest Secret. ISBN 9781603865579

18 Source: Zunin, L. & Zunin, N. (1972). Contact: The First Four Minutes. New York: Balantine Books.

19 Source: Albert Mehrablan, 7-38-55 Communication Model – 'Nonverbal Communi cation'.

20 The field of behavioral economics includes Nobel Prize winners Richard Thaler and Daniel Kahneman, who wrote about the psychology of decision making and fast and slow thinking, e.g. D. Kahneman, Thinking, fast and slow.

21 See: Demand of the Day: Pharrell Williams Must Have a Framed Picture of Carl Sagan in His Dressing Room, and The Daily What - Daily Dose of WHAT? (cheezburger.com).

22 Source: https://gdpr.eu/what-is-gdpr/

23 Source: Andrea Soriani, former Head of Marketing at Maserati North America